MICHELANGELO

the Sculptor

VOLUME II: PLATES, INDEXES

MICHELANGELO
the Sculptor

MARTIN WEINBERGER

Volume II: Plates, Indexes

LONDON: ROUTLEDGE & KEGAN PAUL

NEW YORK: COLUMBIA UNIVERSITY PRESS

First published 1967
by Routledge and Kegan Paul Ltd
Broadway House, 68–74 Carter Lane, London, E.C.4
and Columbia University Press, Columbia University, New York

Copyright © 1967 by Edith Weinberger

Library of Congress Catalog Card Number 65–22158

Printed in Great Britain
Text by William Clowes and Sons, Limited, London and Beccles
Plates by Headley Brothers Limited, The Invicta Press, Ashford, Kent

Contents

LIST OF PLATES   *page* vii

PLATES 1 — 144

A MEMOIR OF THE AUTHOR, BY ULRICH MIDDELDORF   407

WORKS BY MARTIN WEINBERGER   411

INDEXES

INDEX OF WORKS BY MICHELANGELO   417

GENERAL INDEX   423

v

List of Plates

1.1 GIOTTO. *Resurrection of St. John the Evangelist*, detail. Fresco. [Florence, San Croce.]

1.2 MICHELANGELO. Study after Giotto. Pen and ink. [Louvre.]

2.1 MICHELANGELO. Study of three standing figures. Pen and ink. [Vienna, Albertina.]

2.2 MICHELANGELO. Study of a kneeling figure. Pen and ink. [Vienna, Albertina.]

2.3 Florentine, early sixteenth century. Study of three standing figures. Pen and ink. [Florence, Casa Buonarroti.]

2.4 BASTIANO MAINARDI. Study of a kneeling figure. Brush drawing. [Florence, Uffizi.]

3.1 DOMENICO GHIRLANDAIO. Study of two women. Pen and ink. [Florence, Uffizi.]

3.2 MASACCIO. *The Tribute Money*, detail. Fresco. [Florence, Brancacci Chapel.]

3.3 MICHELANGELO. *St. Peter*, after Masaccio's *Tribute Money*. Pen and ink. [Munich, Print Room.]

4.1 BERTOLDO DI GIOVANNI. *Crucifixion*. Bronze relief. [Florence, Bargello.]

4.2 DONATELLO. *Crucifixion*. Bronze relief. [Florence, Bargello.]

5.1 BERTOLDO DI GIOVANNI. *Bellerophon and Pegasus*. Bronze statuette. [Vienna, Kunsthistorisches Museum.]

5.2 BERTOLDO DI GIOVANNI. *Arion*. Bronze statuette. [Florence, Bargello.]

5.3 MICHELANGELO. *Battle of Centaurs*, detail. Marble relief. [Florence, Casa Buonarroti.]

6.1 BERTOLDO DI GIOVANNI. *Battle of Horsemen*. Bronze relief. [Florence, Bargello.]

6.2 Roman sarcophagus. *Battle between Romans and Barbarians*. Marble. [Pisa, Camposanto.]

7.1 BERTOLDO DI GIOVANNI. *Wild Man on Horseback*. Bronze statuette. [Modena, Galleria Estense.]

7.2 DONATELLO. Doors of the Old Sacristy, detail. Bronze. [Florence, San Lorenzo.]

8.1 DESIDERIO DA SETTIGNANO. *Madonna and Child*. Marble relief. [London, Victoria and Albert Museum.]

8.2 DONATELLO. *Madonna in the Clouds*. Marble relief. [Courtesy, Museum of Fine Arts, Boston.]

9 MICHELANGELO. *Madonna of the Stairs*. Marble relief. [Florence, Casa Buonarroti.]

10 MICHELANGELO. *Battle of Centaurs*. Marble relief. [Florence, Casa Buonarroti.]

11.1 ISRAEL SILVESTRE. View of the Cour de la Fontaine at Fontainebleau, detail. Etching. [Courtesy, Metropolitan Museum of Art, New York.]

11.2 ISRAEL SILVESTRE. Title page to a series of views of Fontainebleau. Etching. [Courtesy, Metropolitan Museum of Art, New York.]

11.3 SCHOOL OF GHIRLANDAIO. Drawing after a statue of Hercules of the Farnese type. [From the *Codex Escorialensis*.]

11.4 BERTOLDO DI GIOVANNI. *Hercules*. Bronze statuette. [The Hague, J. W. Frederiks Collection.]

12.1 MICHELANGELO. *St. Petronius*. Marble. [Bologna, San Domenico.]

12.2 MICHELANGELO. *St. Proculus*. Marble. [Bologna, San Domenico.]

13.1 ANDREA VERROCCHIO. *General Bartolommeo Colleoni*, head. Bronze. [Venice, Piazza SS. Giovanni e Paolo.]

13.2 MICHELANGELO. *St. Proculus*, head.

13.3 JACOPO DELLA QUERCIA. *St. Petronius*. Marble. [Bologna, San Petronio.]

13.4 BENEDETTO DA MAIANO. *Madonna and Child*. Marble. [Florence, Misericordia.]

13.5 NICCOLÒ DELL'ARCA. *St. Vitalis*. Marble. [Bologna, San Domenico.]

14.1 NICCOLÒ DELL'ARCA. *Angel*. Marble. [Bologna, San Domenico.]

14.2 MICHELANGELO. *Angel*. [Bologna, San Domenico.]

15.1 DOMENICO GHIRLANDAIO. *The Naming of St. John the Baptist*, detail. Fresco. [Florence, Santa Maria Novella.]

15.2 MICHELANGELO. *Man in a Long Cloak*. Pen and ink with bistre. [By permission, Trustees of the British Museum.]

16 MICHELANGELO. *Bacchus*. Marble. [Florence, Bargello.]

17 MICHELANGELO. *Bacchus*, head.

18.1 MICHELANGELO. *Bacchus*, rear view.

18.2 MICHELANGELO. *Bacchus*, three-quarter view.

19.1 MICHELANGELO. Studies of various figures. Pen and ink. [Chantilly, Musée Condé.]

19.2 MARTEEN VAN HEEMSKERCK. View of Michelangelo's *Bacchus*. Pen and ink. [West Berlin, State Museum.]

19.3 BENEDETTO DA MAIANO. Tomb of Filippo Strozzi. [Florence, Santa Maria Novella.]

20 MICHELANGELO. *Pietà*. Marble. [Rome, St. Peter's.]

21 FILIPPINO LIPPI. Studies for a Pietà. Pen and ink. [1. Louvre. 2 and 3. Cambridge, Mass., Courtesy of the Fogg Art Museum, Harvard University, Bequest of Charles A. Loeser.]

22.1 ANDREA VERROCCHIO. *Faith*, from the Forteguerri Monument. Marble. [From Clarence Kennedy et al., *The Unfinished Monument by Andrea del Verrocchio to the Cardinal Niccolò Forteguerri at Pistoia*, Vol. 7 of Studies in the Criticism of Sculpture (Northampton, Mass., Smith College, 1932), Fig. 7.]

22.2 MICHELANGELO. The Madonna of the *Pietà*, head.

22.3 VERROCCHIO. *Faith*, head. [From Kennedy et al., *The Unfinished Monument*, Plate XXIII.]

22.4 MICHELANGELO. The Christ of the *Pietà*, head.

23.1 NANNI DI BANCO. *Isaiah*. Marble. [Florence Cathedral.]

23.2 DONATELLO. *David*. Marble. [Florence, Bargello.]

24 MICHELANGELO. *David*. Marble. [Florence, Academy.]

25.1 Roman. *The Horsetamers*. Marble. [Rome, Piazza del Quirinale.]

25.2 Roman, second century A.D. *Antinous*. Marble. [Siena, Palazzo Elci.]

25.3 Donatello's *David* in reverse with Michelangelo's *David* superimposed.

25.4 ANTONIO FEDERIGHI. *Bacchus*. Marble. [Siena, Palazzo Elci.]

26.1 MICHELANGELO. Anatomical drawings. Pen and ink. [By permission, Ashmolean Museum, Oxford.]

26.2 MICHELANGELO. *David*, rear view.

27.1 MICHELANGELO. Anatomical studies. Pen and ink. [Louvre.]

27.2 MICHELANGELO. Anatomical studies. Pen and ink. [By permission, Ashmolean Museum, Oxford.]

28.1 MICHELANGELO. *St. Peter*, Piccolomini altar. Marble. [Siena Cathedral.]

28.2 MICHELANGELO. *St. Paul*, Piccolomini altar. Marble. [Siena Cathedral.]

28.3 DONATELLO. *St. Mark*. Marble. [Florence, Or San Michele.]

29.1 MICHELANGELO. *St. Gregory*, Piccolomini altar. Marble. [Siena Cathedral.]

29.2 MICHELANGELO. *St. Pius*, Piccolomini altar. Marble. [Siena Cathedral.]

29.3 NICCOLÒ CORDIERI. *St. Gregory*. Marble. [Rome, San Gregorio Magno.]

30.1 MICHELANGELO. Drawing for the bronze *David*. Pen and ink. [Louvre.]

30.2 Clay model for the reconstruction of the bronze *David*, three-quarter view.

30.3   Clay model for the reconstruction of the bronze *David*, front view.

31.1   MICHELANGELO. Study for a battle scene and of a standing figure. Pen and ink. [By permission, Trustees of the British Museum.]

31.2   MICHELANGELO. Architectural studies. Pen and ink. [By permission, Trustees of the British Museum.]

32.1   MICHELANGELO and pupil. Study for a Madonna and Child. Pen and ink. [West Berlin, State Museum.]

32.2   MICHELANGELO. Study for the Doni *Madonna*. Red chalk. [Florence, Casa Buonarroti.]

32.3   LUCA SIGNORELLI. *Holy Family*. Tempera. [Florence, Uffizi.]

32.4   LUCA SIGNORELLI. *Madonna and Child*. Tempera. [Florence, Uffizi.]

33   MICHELANGELO. Doni *Madonna*. Tempera. [Florence, Uffizi.]

34   MICHELANGELO. Taddei *Madonna*. Marble relief. [London, Royal Academy.]

35   MICHELANGELO. Pitti *Madonna*. Marble relief. [Florence, Bargello.]

36   MICHELANGELO. *Delphic Sibyl*, detail of the Sistine ceiling. Fresco. [Vatican, Sistine Chapel.]

37.1   DONATELLO. *Judith and Holofernes*. Bronze. [Florence, Piazza della Signoria.]

37.2   MICHELANGELO. *Madonna and Child*. [Bruges, Church of Notre Dame, Copyright A.C.L. Brussels.]

38.1   MICHELANGELO. Bruges *Madonna*, head, front view.

38.2   MICHELANGELO. Madonna of the *Pietà*, head, front view.

38.3   MICHELANGELO. *St. Peter*, head, front view. Piccolomini altar. [Siena Cathedral.]

38.4   MICHELANGELO. *St. Pius*, head, front view. Piccolomini altar. [Siena Cathedral.]

39.1   DONATELLO. *Judith*, head, front view.

39.2   MICHELANGELO. Pitti *Madonna*, head.

39.3   MICHELANGELO. Bruges *Madonna*, head, profile. [Copyright A.C.L. Brussels.]

39.4   MICHELANGELO. *St. Pius*, head, profile. Piccolomini altar. [Siena Cathedral.]

40.1   MICHELANGELO. *St. Anne with the Virgin*. Pen and ink. [Louvre.]

40.2   MICHELANGELO. *St. Anne with the Virgin*. [By permission, Ashmolean Museum, Oxford.]

41.1   MICHELANGELO. Study of a beckoning youth. Pen and ink. [By permission, Trustees of the British Museum.]

41.2   MICHELANGELO. Studies of children. Pen and ink. [By permission, Trustees of the British Museum.]

42.1   MICHELANGELO. Studies for the *Battle of Cascina*. Black chalk. [By permission, Trustees of the British Museum.]

42.2 ARISTOTILE DA SANGALLO. Copy of the *Battle of Cascina*. Grisaille. [Leicester Collection, Holkham Hall, Norfolk.]

43.1 MICHELANGELO. Studies for the *Battle of Cascina* and the Taddei *Madonna*. Black chalk. [By permission, Trustees of the British Museum.]

43.2 LUCA SIGNORELLI. Study for a figure in the *Flagellation*. Black chalk. [Louvre.]

43.3 MICHELANGELO AND PUPIL. Studies for the *Battle of Cascina* and for Madonnas. Black chalk. [Florence, Uffizi.]

44.1 MICHELANGELO. Studies after the antique. Pen and ink on parchment. [Louvre.]

44.2 MICHELANGELO. Apollonian youth. Pen and ink. [Louvre.]

44.3 Greek, fifth century B.C., restored by Alessandro Algardi. *Hermes Ludovisi*. Marble. [Vatican.]

44.4 SCHOOL OF RAPHAEL. Study of Mercury. Pen and ink. [Devonshire Collection, Chatsworth, Derbyshire. Reproduced by permission of the Trustees of the Chatsworth Settlement.]

45.1 MICHELANGELO. Studies for the Bruges *Madonna* and a Mercury. Pen and ink on parchment. [Louvre.]

45.2 MICHELANGELO. Study for a Captive. Black chalk. [Uffizi.]

45.3 MICHELANGELO. Study after the *David*. Pen and ink. [Louvre, © S.P.A.D.E.M., Paris, 1964.]

46 MICHELANGELO. *St. Matthew*. Marble. [Florence, Academy.]

47.1 MICHELANGELO. *St. Matthew*, head.

47.2 MICHELANGELO. Head of a man. Pen and ink with bistre. [Louvre.]

47.3 JACOPO SANSOVINO. *St. James*. Marble. [Florence, Signoria.]

48.1 MICHELANGELO. Bruges *Madonna*, side view. [Copyright A.C.L. Brussels.]

48.2 MICHELANGELO. Study for the Bruges *Madonna*. (See lower right corner; the large figure is the work of a pupil.) [Chantilly, Musée Condé.]

49 MICHELANGELO. Study for the Sistine ceiling with sketches of six Slaves and a cornice. Red chalk. [By permission, Ashmolean Museum, Oxford.]

50.1 BARTOLOMEO AMMANATI. *Victory* for the tomb of Mario Nari. Marble. [Florence, Bargello.]

50.2 BENEDETTO DA ROVESSANO AND OTHERS. Tomb of Charles d'Orléans. Marble. [Paris, St. Denis.]

50.3 Roman sarcophagus. Marble. [Vatican, Belvedere.]

50.4 LORENZO GHIBERTI. *Deborah*, detail of the Doors of Paradise. Bronze. [Florence, Baptistery.]

51.1 SCHOOL OF MICHELANGELO. Copy of drawing for the Tomb of Julius II. Pen and ink. [East Berlin, State Museum.]

51.2   MICHELANGELO. Drawing for the Tomb of Julius II. Pen and ink. [Florence, Uffizi.]

52.1   MICHELANGELO. *Rebellious Slave*. Marble. [Louvre.]

52.2   MICHELANGELO. *Dying Slave*. Marble. [Louvre.]

53.1   MICHELANGELO. Detail of the Sistine ceiling. Fresco. [Vatican, Sistine Chapel.]

53.2   SCHOOL OF MICHELANGELO. Copy of a study for a Slave. Pen and ink. [Paris, École des Beaux-Arts.]

54.1   MICHELANGELO. *Dying Slave*, three-quarter view. [From Ludwig Goldscheider, *Michelangelo: Paintings, Sculptures, Architecture* (4th ed., London, Phaidon Press, 1962), Plate 152.]

54.2   Greek, first century B.C. *Laocoön*. Marble. [Vatican, Belvedere.]

54.3   Greek, *ca.* 300 B.C. *Dead Niobid*. Marble. [Munich, Glyptothek.]

55   MICHELANGELO. *Moses*, Tomb of Julius II. Marble. [Rome, San Pietro in Vincoli.]

56.1   DONATELLO. *St. John the Evangelist*. Marble. [Florence, Duomo.]

56.2   MICHELANGELO. *Rebellious Slave*, three-quarter view.

57.1   MICHELANGELO. *Rebellious Slave*, front view.

57.2   MICHELANGELO. *Moses*, three-quarter view.

58.1   MICHELANGELO. *Christ*. Marble. [Rome, Santa Maria sopra Minerva.]

58.2   MICHELANGELO. *Christ*, side view.

59.1   MICHELANGELO. *Christ*, three-quarter view.

59.2   MICHELANGELO. Study for *Christ*. Pen and ink over red chalk. [London, Brinsley Ford Collection.]

59.3   SCHOOL OF MICHELANGELO. Studies of legs. Pen and ink, verso of drawing in Plate 59.2.

60.1   MICHELANGELO. *Youthful Captive*. Marble. [Florence, Academy.]

60.2   MICHELANGELO. *Atlas*. Marble. [Florence, Academy.]

61.1   MICHELANGELO. *Awakening Captive*. Marble. [Florence, Academy.]

61.2   MICHELANGELO. *Bearded Captive*. Marble. [Florence, Academy.]

62.1   MICHELANGELO. *Atlas*, side view.

62.2   MICHELANGELO. *Awakening Captive*, side view.

63.1   SCHOOL OF MICHELANGELO. Model after a Slave. Wax. [Florence, Casa Buonarroti.]

63.2   MICHELANGELO. Model for the *Youthful Captive*. Wax. [London, Victoria and Albert Museum.]

64.1   MICHELANGELO. Model for the *Youthful Captive*, left side view.

64.2   MICHELANGELO. Model for the *Youthful Captive*, right side view.

65.1   PIETRO URBANO. *St. Sebastian*. Marble. [London, Victoria and Albert Museum.]

65.2   MICHELANGELO. Model for the *Youthful Captive*, rear view.

66.1 MICHELANGELO. Architectural sketches for the Tomb of Julius II. Pen and ink. [By permission, Trustees of the British Museum.]

66.2 MICHELANGELO. Rendering of projected tabernacle for San Silvestro in Capite. Pen and ink. [Florence, Casa Buonarroti.]

66.3 MICHELANGELO AND PUPIL. Architectural working drawing. Pen and ink. [By permission, the Governing Body of Christ Church, Oxford.]

67.1 MICHELANGELO. Study for the Tomb of Julius II. Pen and ink. [By permission, Trustees of the British Museum.]

67.2 MICHELANGELO. Estimates of marble for Tomb of Julius II, verso of drawing in Plate 67.1. [By permission, Trustees of the British Museum.]

67.3 ANDREA FERRUCCI. Tabernacle for San Girolamo, Fiesole. Marble. [London, Victoria and Albert Museum.]

67.4 MICHELANGELO. Study for a statue of the Pope, Tomb of Julius II. Pen and ink. [Florence, Casa Buonarroti.]

68.1 MICHELANGELO. Faces of satyrs with sketch of Hercules. Red chalk. [By permission, Trustees of the British Museum.]

68.2 SCHOOL OF MICHELANGELO. Various sketches, including two of Hercules. [By permission, Ashmolean Museum, Oxford.]

69.1 BACCIO BANDINELLI. *Hercules and Cacus.* Wax model. [East Berlin, State Museum.]

69.2 MICHELANGELO. Drawing of two struggling figures. [Florence, Casa Buonarroti.

70 MICHELANGELO. *Samson and Two Philistines.* Bronze cast. [Florence, Bargello.]

71.1 DANIELE DA VOLTERRA. *Slaughter of the Innocents,* detail. Fresco. [Florence, Uffizi.]

71.2 MICHELANGELO. *Samson and Two Philistines.* Bronze cast. [West Berlin, State Museum.]

72.1 BACCIO BANDINELLI. *Hercules and Cacus.* Marble. [Florence, Piazza della Signoria.]

72.2 BACCIO BANDINELLI. *Hercules and Cacus.* Pen and ink. [Florence, Uffizi.]

73.1 MICHELANGELO. Model of two fighting men, right profile view. Clay. [Florence, Casa Buonarroti.]

73.2 MICHELANGELO. Model of two fighting men, rear view.

74 MICHELANGELO. *Victory.* Marble. [Florence, Palazzo Vecchio.]

75 MICHELANGELO. Model of two fighting men, main view.

76.1 PIERINO DA VINCI. *Samson and a Philistine.* Marble. [Florence, Palazzo Vecchio.]

76.2 VINCENZO DANTI. *Honor Overcoming Deceit.* Marble. [Florence, Bargello.]

76.3 MICHELANGELO. Study for the *Last Judgment.* Pen and ink. [Louvre.]

77.1 MICHELANGELO. Study of the *Virgin Annunciate.* Black chalk. [By permission, Trustees of the British Museum.]

77.2 MICHELANGELO. Study of a torso. Black chalk. [By permission, Trustees of the British Museum.]

78 MICHELANGELO. *Rachel*, Tomb of Julius II. Marble. [Rome, San Pietro in Vincoli.]

79 MICHELANGELO. *Leah*, Tomb of Julius II. Marble. [Rome, San Pietro in Vincoli.]

80 MICHELANGELO. Tomb of Julius II, lower half. [Rome, San Pietro in Vincoli.]

81.1 ARISTOTILE DA SANGALLO. Architectural drawing for the Tomb of Julius II. Pen and ink. [Florence, Uffizi.]

81.2 MICHELANGELO. Tomb of Julius II. [Rome, San Pietro in Vincoli.]

82 MICHELANGELO. The Medici Chapel. [Florence, San Lorenzo.]

83.1 MICHELANGELO. Early sketch for the Medici Chapel (lower left corner). Red chalk. (Superimposed on an earlier anonymous sketch and estimate.) [Florence, Archivio Buonarroti.]

83.2 MICHELANGELO. Architectural drawing for the Medici Chapel. Red chalk, verso of drawing in Plate 83.1. [From Tolnay, *Michelangelo*, Vol. III, Plate 79, by permission of the author and Princeton University Press.]

84.1 MICHELANGELO. Architectural studies for the Medici Chapel. Pen and ink. [Florence, Casa Buonarroti.]

84.2 MICHELANGELO. Architectural study for the Medici Chapel. Pen and ink. [Florence, Casa Buonarroti.]

84.3 MICHELANGELO. Architectural study for the Medici Chapel. Black chalk. [By permission, Trustees of the British Museum.]

85.1 MICHELANGELO. Architectural study for the Medici Chapel. Black chalk. [By permission, Trustees of the British Museum.]

85.2 MICHELANGELO. Architectural study for the Medici Chapel. Black chalk, verso of the drawing on Plate 85.1. [By permission, Trustees of the British Museum.]

86 LORENZO GHIBERTI. Biblical figures, details of the Doors of Paradise. 1. 'Eve.' 2. 'Adam.' 3. 'Noah.' 4. 'Noah's Wife.' Bronze. [Florence, Baptistery.]

87.1 MICHELANGELO. Study for a wall tomb of the Medici Chapel. Black chalk. [By permission, Trustees of the British Museum.]

87.2 MICHELANGELO. Architectural studies for the Medici Chapel. Red chalk. [Florence, Casa Buonarroti.]

88.1 SILVIO COSINI. Trophy for the Medici Chapel. Marble. [Florence, San Lorenzo.]

88.2 SILVIO COSINI. Trophy for the Medici Chapel. Marble. [Florence, San Lorenzo.]

88.3 SILVIO COSINI. Tomb of Ruggiero Minerbetti, detail. Marble. [Rome, Santa Maria Novella.]

89.1 ANDREA FERRUCCI. Tomb of Antonio Strozzi. Marble. [Rome, Santa Maria Novella.]

89.2   SILVIO COSINI. Candelabrum for the Medici Chapel. Marble. [Florence, San Lorenzo.

89.3   SILVIO COSINI. Frieze for the Medici Chapel, detail. Marble. [Florence, San Lorenzo.]

90.1   MICHELANGELO. Architectural study for the Medici Chapel. Pen and ink. [By permission, Trustees of the British Museum.]

90.2   MICHELANGELO. Architectural study for the Medici Chapel. Pen and ink, verso of the drawing in Plate 90.1. [By permission, Trustees of the British Museum.]

91   MICHELANGELO. *Madonna and Child*. Medici Chapel. Marble. [Florence, San Lorenzo.]

92.1   Medici Chapel, wall niche.

92.2   MICHELANGELO. Study for a wall niche in the Medici Chapel. Pen and ink. [Florence, Casa Buonarroti.]

93   The Medici Chapel, diagonal view.

94.1   ARISTOTILE DA SANGALLO. Sketch for the Medici Chapel. Pen and ink with bistre. [Florence, Uffizi.]

94.2   SCHOOL OF MICHELANGELO. Study for the Medici Chapel after Aristotile da Sangallo. Black chalk with bistre. [Louvre.]

95.1   SCHOOL OF MICHELANGELO. Study of a wall tomb in the Medici Chapel. Pen and ink. [Louvre.]

95.2   SCHOOL OF MICHELANGELO. Study of a wall tomb in the Medici Chapel. Black chalk. [By permission, Ashmolean Museum, Oxford.]

96.1   MICHELANGELO. Study for *Night*. Black chalk. [Florence, Uffizi.]

96.2   MICHELANGELO. Study for *Night*. Black chalk, verso of the drawing in Plate 96.1.

96.3   MICHELANGELO. Study for *Night*. Black chalk. [Florence, Uffizi.]

96.4   MICHELANGELO. Study of legs. Black chalk. [Florence, Casa Buonarroti.]

97.1   MICHELANGELO. Study for *Day*. Black chalk. [By permission, Ashmolean Museum, Oxford.]

97.2   MICHELANGELO. Study for right leg of *Lorenzo*. Black chalk. [By permission, Trustees of the British Museum.]

97.3   MICHELANGELO. Studies for the right arm of *Night*. Red chalk. [By permission, Ashmolean Museum, Oxford.]

97.4   MICHELANGELO. Studies for *Night* and for *Giuliano*. Pen and ink. [Florence, Casa Buonarroti.]

98.1   MICHELANGELO. Study for *Day*. Black chalk. [By permission, Ashmolean Museum, Oxford.]

98.2   MICHELANGELO. Study for *Day*. Black chalk. [By permission, Ashmolean Museum, Oxford.]

99.1   MICHELANGELO. Model for a River God. Clay. [Florence, Academy.]

99.2   MARTEEN VAN HEEMSKERCK. View of the Belvedere torso. Pen and ink. [West Berlin, State Museum.]

100.1 MICHELANGELO. *Night*, Medici Chapel. Marble. [Florence, San Lorenzo.]

100.2 APOLLONIOS OF ATHENS, second century B.C. Torso. Marble. [Vatican, Belvedere.]

101.1 MICHELANGELO. *Day*, Medici Chapel. Marble. [Florence, San Lorenzo.]

101.2 MICHELANGELO. Model for a River God, side view. [Florence. Academy.]

102.1 MICHELANGELO. *Evening*, Medici Chapel. Marble. [Florence, San Lorenzo.]

102.2 MICHELANGELO. *Day*, rear view.

102.3 MICHELANGELO. *Evening*, rear view.

103.1 MICHELANGELO. *Dawn*, Medici Chapel. Marble. [Florence, San Lorenzo.]

103.2 MICHELANGELO. *Dawn*, rear view.

103.3 MICHELANGELO. *Night*, rear view.

104   MICHELANGELO. *Lorenzo*, Medici Chapel. Marble. [Florence, San Lorenzo.]

105   MICHELANGELO. *Giuliano*, Medici Chapel. Marble. [Florence, San Lorenzo.]

106   Tomb of *Lorenzo*, Medici Chapel.

107   Tomb of *Giuliano*, Medici Chapel.

108.1 MICHELANGELO. *Night*, head. [Florence, San Lorenzo.]

108.2 MICHELANGELO. Madonna of the Medici Chapel, detail of head. [Florence, San Lorenzo.

108.3 MICHELANGELO. *Dawn*, head. Medici Chapel.

109.1 MICHELANGELO. Madonna of the Medici Chapel, profile.

109.2 MICHELANGELO. *Dawn*, profile.

109.3 Tomb of Giuliano, Mask, from *Night*.

110.1 MICHELANGELO. *David*, head. [Florence, Academy.]

110.2 MICHELANGELO. *Victory*, profile. [Florence, Palazzo, Vecchio.

110.3 MICHELANGELO. *Giuliano*, profile. [Florence, San Lorenzo.]

110.4 MICHELANGELO. *Night*, profile. [Florence, San Lorenzo.]

111.1 MICHELANGELO. *Victory*, head. [Florence, Palazzo Vecchio.]

111.2 MICHELANGELO. *Giuliano*, head. [Florence, San Lorenzo.]

111.3 MICHELANGELO. *Evening*, head. [Florence, San Lorenzo.]

111.4 MICHELANGELO. *Lorenzo*, head. [Florence, San Lorenzo.]

112.1 MICHELANGELO. *Brutus*. Marble. [Florence, Bargello.]

112.2 GIOVANNANTONIO MONTORSOLI. Tomb of Jacopo Sannazaro. Marble. [Naples, Santa Maria del Parto.]

113.1 MICHELANGELO. *Lorenzo*, rear view. [Florence, San Lorenzo.]

113.2 MICHELANGELO. *Giuliano*, rear view. [Florence, San Lorenzo.]

113.3 BARTOLOMEO AMMANATI. *Earth*. Marble. [Florence, Palazzo Vecchio.]

113.4 SCHOOL OF MICHELANGELO. '*Sepoltura del duca Lorenzo*.' Pen and ink with bistre. [Vienna, Albertina.]

113.5 GIORGIO VASARI. Portrait of Alessandro de'Medici. Oil. [Florence, Museo Mediceo.]

114.1 MICHELANGELO. *Earth*. Clay model. [Florence, Casa Buonarroti.]

114.2 *Earth*, left side view.

115.1 *Earth*, rear view.

115.2 *Earth*, right side view.

116.1 SCHOOL OF MICHELANGELO. Study of a model for *Heaven*, front view. Pen and ink. [Louvre.]

116.2 SCHOOL OF MICHELANGELO. Study of a model for *Heaven*, left side view. Pen and ink, verso of the drawing in Plate 116.1. [Louvre.]

117.1 Reconstruction of *Heaven*, from the drawings on Plate 116.

117.2 Reconstruction of *Heaven*, side view.

117.3 BENVENUTO CELLINI. *Mercury*, detail of the pedestal of *Perseus*. Bronze. [Florence, Loggia dei Lanzi.]

117.4 SCHOOL OF GIAMBOLOGNA. *Mercury with the Head of Argus*. [Munich, Bavarian National Museum.]

117.5 Reconstruction of *Heaven*, main view.

118.1 MICHELANGELO. Study for *Minerva*. Red chalk. [Florence, Casa Buonarroti.]

118.2 BENVENUTO CELLINI. *Minerva*, detail of the pedestal of *Perseus*. Bronze. [Florence, Loggia dei Lanzi.]

118.3 MICHELANGELO. Study for *Minerva*. Black chalk. [Florence, Casa Buonarroti.]

118.4 MICHELANGELO. Study for *Minerva*. Black chalk. [By permission, Trustees of the British Museum.]

118.5 MICHELANGELO. Study for *Minerva*. Black chalk. [By permission, Trustees of the British Museum.]

118.6 MICHELANGELO. Study for *Minerva*. Black chalk, recto of the drawing in Plate 118.3. [Florence, Casa Buonarroti.]

119.1 SCHOOL OF MICHELANGELO. Study of *Apollo*. Red chalk. [Florence, Casa Buonarroti.]

119.2 SCHOOL OF MICHELANGELO. Study of a youth. Red chalk. [Florence, Casa Buonarroti.]

119.3 SCHOOL OF MICHELANGELO. Study of *Apollo*. Pen and ink. [Louvre.]

xvii

119.4 FRANCESCO SALVIATI. Study of *Apollo*. Pen and ink. [Vienna, Albertina.]

120 MICHELANGELO. *Apollo*. Marble. [Florence, Bargello.]

121.1 MICHELANGELO. *Apollo*, right side view.

121.2 MICHELANGELO. *Apollo*, left side view.

122.1 MICHELANGELO. Study of a Dragon. [By permission, Ashmolean Museum, Oxford.]

122.2 SCHOOL OF MICHELANGELO. Copy of the drawing on Plate 122.1. Pen and ink. [Louvre.]

123.1 MICHELANGELO. Study for *Isaiah*. Pen and ink with bistre. [By permission, Trustees of the British Museum.]

123.2 MICHELANGELO AND PUPIL. Head of a Satyr. Pen and ink over red chalk. [Louvre.]

124.1 MICHELANGELO. Model for a River God. Clay. [Florence, Academy.]

124.2 SCHOOL OF MICHELANGELO. Model for a River God. Wax. [By permission, Trustees of the British Museum.]

124.3 Roman. *Okeanos*. Marble. [Venice, Museo Archeologico.]

125.1 MICHELANGELO. Study of legs. Pen and ink. [Florence, Casa Buonarroti.]

125.2 MICHELANGELO. Study for a River God. Pen and ink. [Bayonne.]

126.1 SCHOOL OF MICHELANGELO. River God. Terra cotta. [London, Victoria and Albert Museum.]

126.2 VINCENZO DANTI. River God for Ammanati's Fountain of Neptune. Bronze. [Florence, Piazza del Signoria.]

127.1 MICHELANGELO. Working drawing for a River God. Pen and ink. [By permission, Trustees of the British Museum.]

127.2 Model of River God based on the working drawing.

128.1 SCHOOL OF MICHELANGELO. Copy of the Academy River God. Bronze. [Florence, Bargello.]

128.2 SCHOOL OF MICHELANGELO. Copy of the Academy River God. Bronze. [Florence, Bargello.]

129.1 VINCENZO DANTI. *Honor Overcoming Deceit*. Marble. [Florence, Bargello.]

129.2 VINCENZO DANTI. Study of a winged Victory. Pen and ink. [Florence, Casa Buonarroti.]

130.1 VINCENZO DANTI. *Cosimo I*. Marble. [Florence, Bargello.]

130.2 VINCENZO DANTI. Statuette of a youth. Bronze. [Amsterdam, Rijksmuseum.]

131.1 VINCENZO DANTI. Statuette after Michelangelo's *Bacchus*. Wax over clay. [Florence, Casa Buonarroti.]

131.2 VINCENZO DANTI. Statuette after *Bacchus*, rear view.

132.1 TRIBOLO. *Victory*. Marble. [Florence, Palazzo Alessandri.]

132.2   TRIBOLO. Statuette of a young man. Clay. [Florence, Casa Buonarroti.]

133.1   TRIBOLO. Medici coat of arms. Marble. [Prato, Palazzo del Commune.]

133.2   TRIBOLO. *Evening*, after Michelangelo. Terra cotta. [Florence, Bargello.]

134.1   MICHELANGELO. *Night*, diagonal view. [Florence, San Lorenzo.]

134.2   SCHOOL OF MICHELANGELO. *Night*, after Michelangelo. Oil. [Rome, Palazzo Colonna.]

135.1   MICHELANGELO. *Day*, diagonal view. [Florence, San Lorenzo.]

135.2   TRIBOLO. *Day*, after Michelangelo. Terra cotta. [Florence, Bargello.]

136.1   Michelangelo. *Dawn*, diagonal view. [Florence, San Lorenzo.]

136.2   TRIBOLO. *Dawn*, after Michelangelo. Terra cotta. [Florence, Bargello.]

137   Reconstructions showing placement of *Day*.

138   Reconstruction. Tomb of *Giuliano* with niche figures of *Earth* and *Heaven*.

139   Reconstruction. Tomb of *Lorenzo* with *Night* and *Day*.

140.1   ANTONIO ROSSELLINO. Tomb of the Cardinal of Portugal, detail. Marble. [Florence, San Miniato.]

140.2   Tomb of the Cardinal of Portugal, detail of frieze.

141.1   DESIDERIO DA SETTIGNANO. Tomb of Carlo Marzuppini, detail. Marble. [Florence, Santa Croce.]

141.2   Roman sarcophagus. Porphyry. [Rome, San Giovanni in Laterano.]

142   MICHELANGELO. Ricetto of the Laurentian Library. [Florence.]

143   The Medici Chapel. View of the side wall. [From Tolnay, *Michelangelo*, Vol. III, Plate 4, by permission of the author and Princeton University Press.]

144   MICHELANGELO. *Crouching Boy*. Marble. [Leningrad, State Hermitage Museum.]

[*Photographs: 1.1, 1.2, 3.2, 4.1, 5.2, 7.1, 13.3, 13.4, 14.2, 15.1, 15.2, 19.3, 20, 22.2, 23.1, 24, 25.1, 28.3, 32.3, 32.4, 34, 36, 38.2, 39.1, 40.1, 41.2, 42.1, 43.2, 44.1, 44.2, 44.3, 47.1, 47.3, 51.2, 52.1, 52.2, 53.1, 54.2, 67.3, 68.1, 70, 71.1, 72.1, 76.2, 76.3, 77.1, 78, 79, 81.1, 89.1, 89.3, 92.1, 96.3, 96.4, 97.4, 104, 105, 106, 107, 109.3, 112.1, 113.3, 113.5, 116.2, 117.3, 118.2, 119.2, 119.3, 120, 123.2, 125.1, 128.1, 128.2, 129.1, 130.1, 131.1, 132.1, 132.2, 133.1, 133.2, 135.1, 136.1, 140.2, 142—Alinari; 2.4, 3.1, 6.1, 43.3, 46, 63.1, 66.2, 69.2, 72.2, 83.1, 88.1, 88.2, 96.1, 96.2, 102.2, 102.3, 103.2, 103.3, 110.1, 111.2, 112.2, 113.1, 113.2, 118.1, 136.2—Soprintendenza alle Gallerie, Florence; 4.2, 5.3, 7.2, 9, 10, 12.1, 12.2, 13.2, 16, 17, 23.2, 26.2, 28.1, 28.2, 29.1, 29.2, 32.2, 33, 35, 38.3, 38.4, 39.2, 39.4, 73.1, 73.2, 76.1, 82, 89.2, 91, 93, 101.2, 103.1, 108.1, 108.2, 108.3, 109.1, 109.2, 110.2, 110.3, 110.4, 111.1, 111.3, 111.4, 119.1, 121.2, 126.2, 129.2, 131.2, 135.2, 140.1, 141.1—Brogi; 6.2—Deutsches Archäologisches Instituts; 13.5, 141—Villani, Bologna; 18.1, 99.1, 124.3—Mannelli; 19.1, 27.1, 45.1, 45.2, 48. 2, 94.2, 95.1—Giraudon; 37.2, 39.3, 48.1—Archives Centrales Iconographiques d'Art National, Brussels; 42.2—Courtald Institute; 45.3, 116.1—Braun; 47.2, 55, 57.2, 58.1, 58.2—Anderson; 131—Kaufmann, Munich; 50.3—L'Archivio Fotografico dei Musei e Gallerie Ponifice; 81.2—Chauffourier, Rome; 88.3, 94.1—Fototeca Italiana, Florence; 100.1, 101.1, 102.1—Cipriani; 119.4—Frankenstein, Vienna; 122.2—Caisse Nationale des Monuments Historiques, Paris; 124.1—Foto Fiorentini, Venice; 125.2—Bulloz, Paris; 141.2—Ministèro della Pubblica Istruzione, Rome. The following photographs were made especially for this book: 21.1, 56.2, 57.1—Giraudon; 37.1—Kunsthistorische Institut, Florence; 59.1—Ministèro della Pubblica Istruzione, Rome; 60.1, 60.2, 61.1, 61.2, 62.1, 62.2, 74, 75, 114.1, 114.2, 114.3, 114.4, 118.3, 118.6, 134.1—Soprintendenza alle Gallerie, Florence. Where a specific source is not given, the photograph was obtained from the museum.*]

PLATES

I.I

I.2

2.1

2.2

2.3

2.4

3.1

3.2

3.3

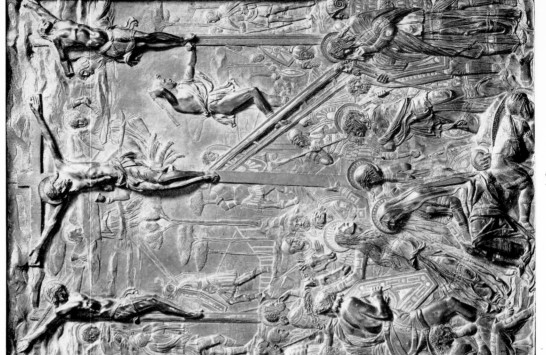

4.2

4.1

5.1

5.2

5.3

7.1

7.2

8.1

8.2

9

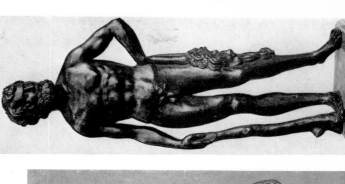

II.1

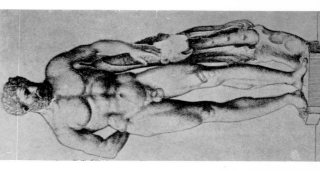

II.3

II.4

Oeuure veue du Chasteau et des bastiments de Fontaine belleau dessiné et graué
par Ihrael Siluestre
Deue du bastiment de la Cour des fontaines, et du
Iardin de l'Estan.

A Paris Chez Ihrael au logis de Monsieur le Mercier Orfeure de la Reyne, rue de l'Arbre sec proche la croix du Tiroir

II.2

12.1

12.2

13.1

13.2

13.3

13.4

13.5

15.1

15.2

16

18.1   18.2

19.1

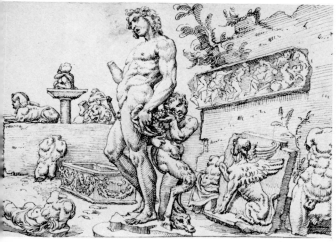

19.2

19.3

21.1

21.2

21.3

22.1

22.2

22.3

22.4

23.1   23.2

24

25.1

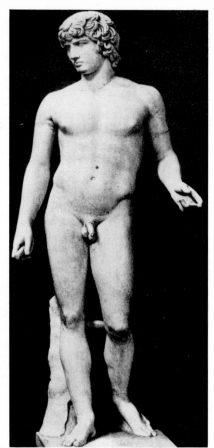

25.2

25.3

25.4

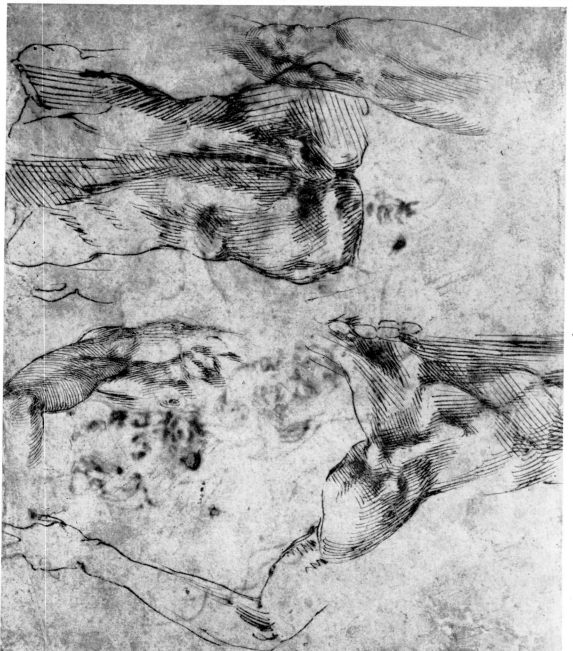

26.1

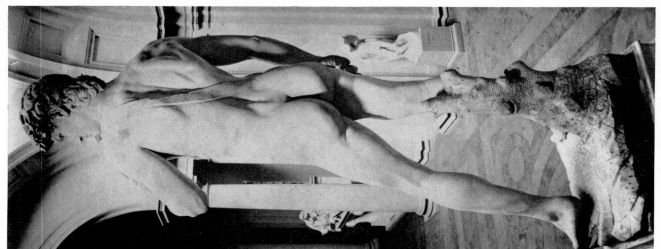

26.2

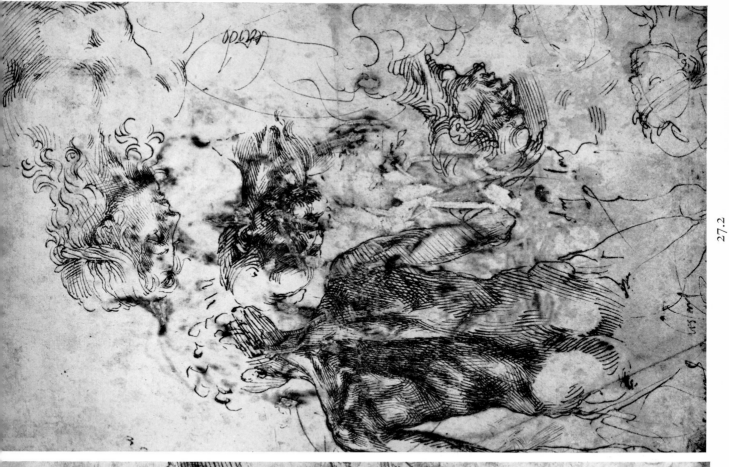

27.2

27.1

28.1

28.2

28.3

29.1

29.2

29.3

30.1

30.2

30.3

31.1

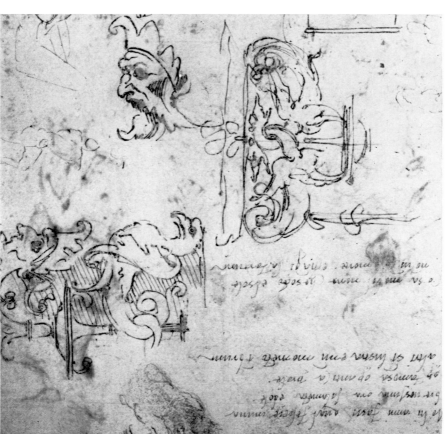

31.2

32.1

32.2

32.3

32.4

33

34

35

DELPHICA

37.1

37.2

38.1

38.2

38.3

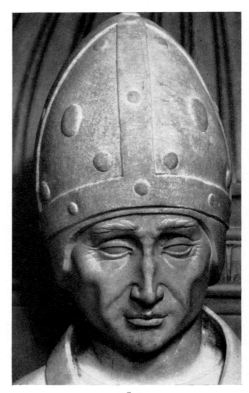

38.4

39.1

39.2

39.3

39.4

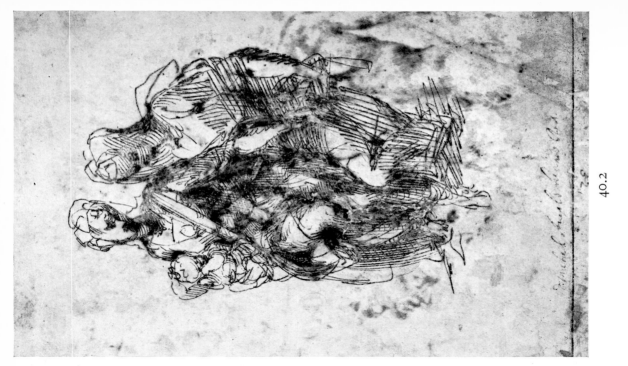

41.1

41.2

42.1

42.2

43.1

43.2

43.3

44.1

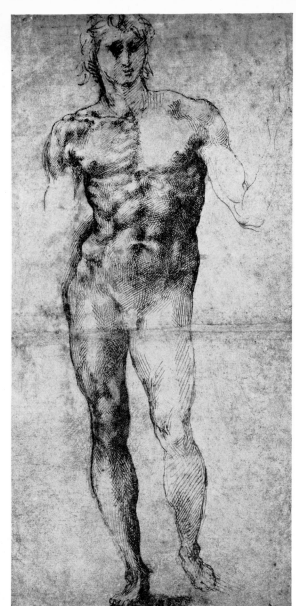

44.2

44.3

44.4

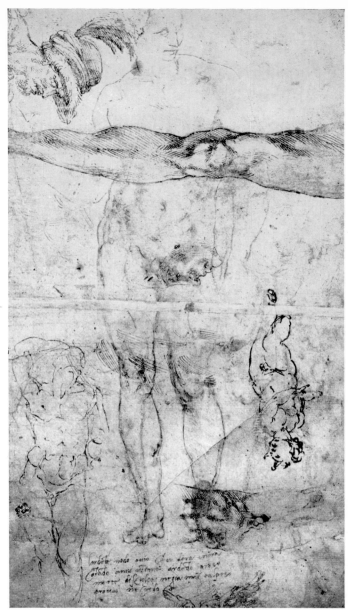

45.1

45.2

45.3

46

47.2

47.3

48.1

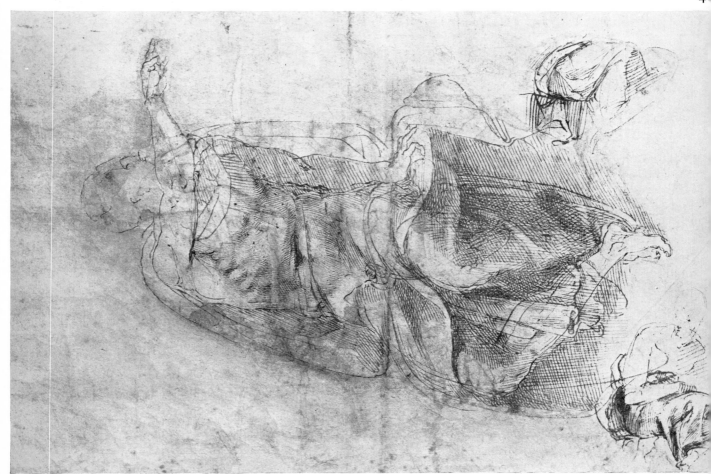

4

49

50.1

50.2

50.3

50.4

51.1

51.2

52.1   52.2

53.1

53.2

54.1

54.2

54.3

56.1

56.2

57.1

57.2

58.1   58.2

59.1

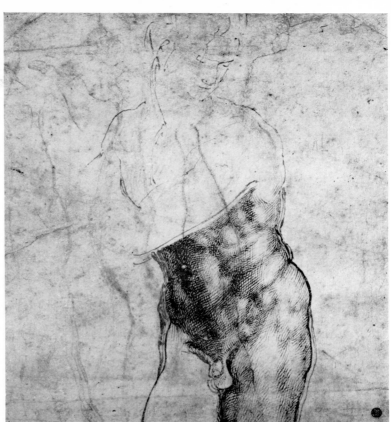

59.2

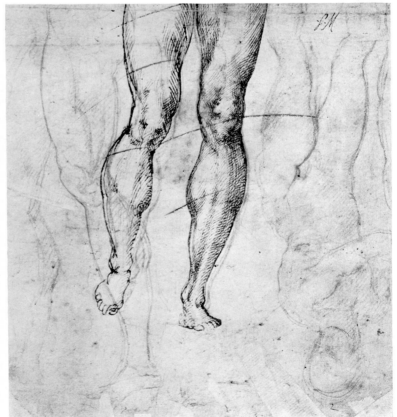

59.3

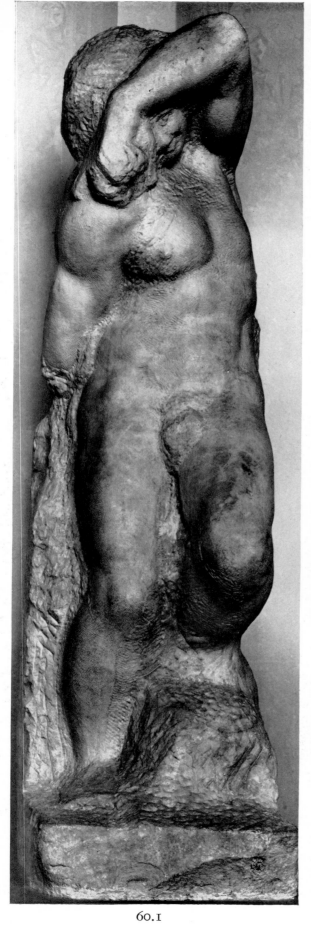

60.1   60.2

61.1

61.2

62.1

62.2

63.1

63.2

64.1   64.2

65.1

65.2

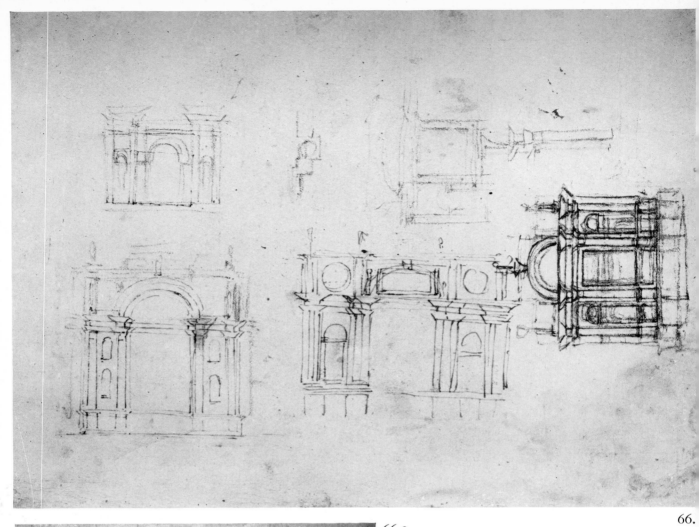

66.

66.2

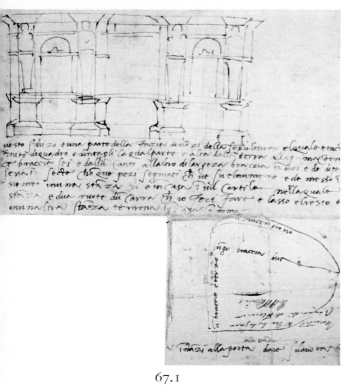

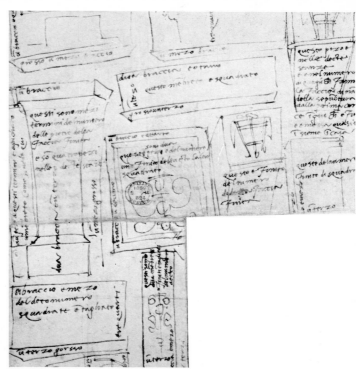

67.1

67.2

67.3

67.4

68.1

68.2

69.1   69.2

70

71.1   71.2

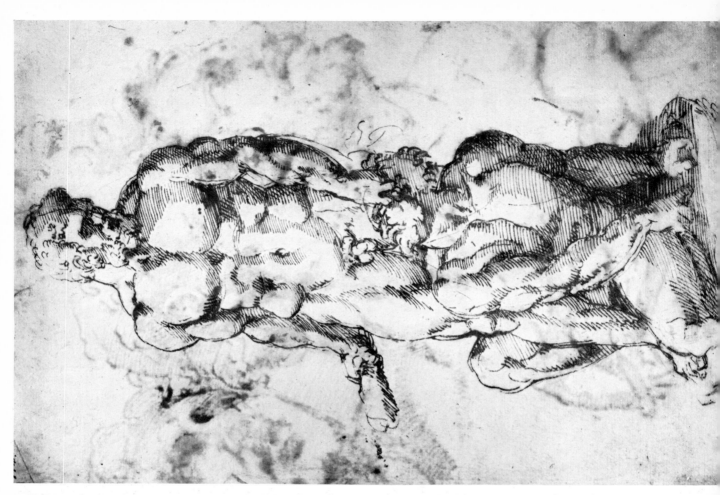

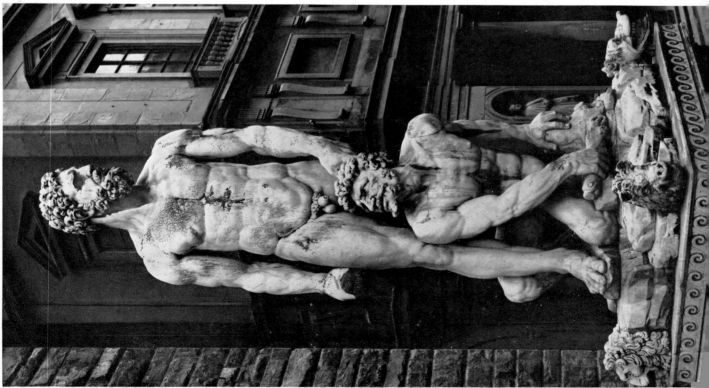

73.2

73.1

74

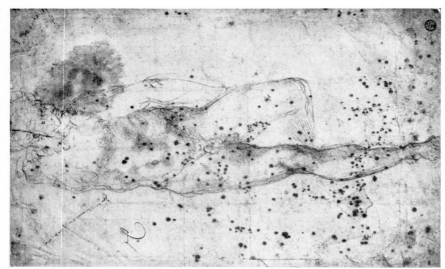

76.3

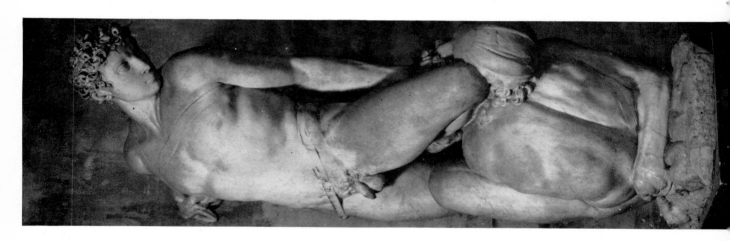

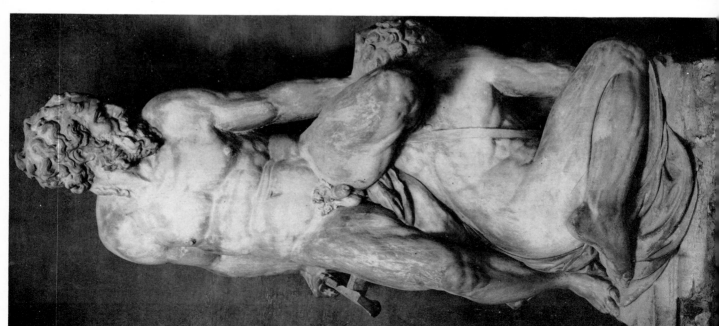

77.2

77.1

78

79

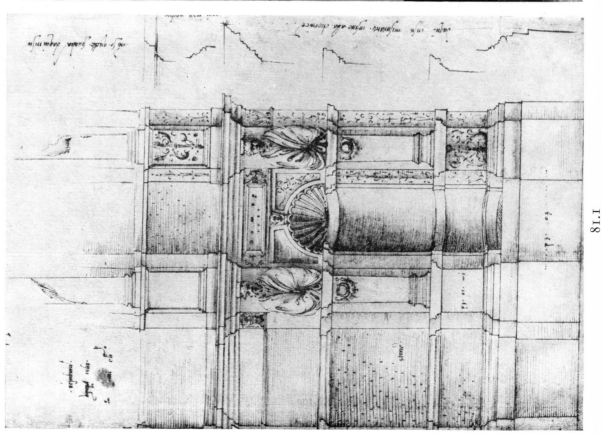

81.1

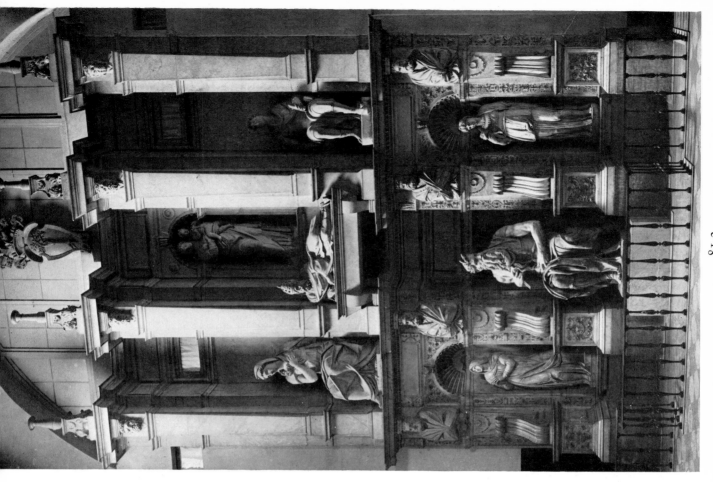

81.2

el braccio deglintonati della capella $ 20

83.1

83.2

84.3

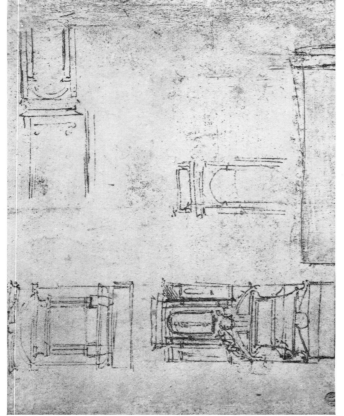

84.1

84.2

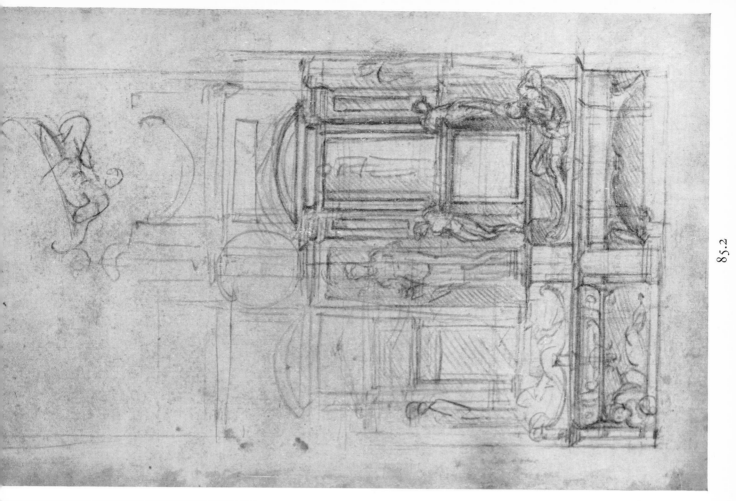

85.1

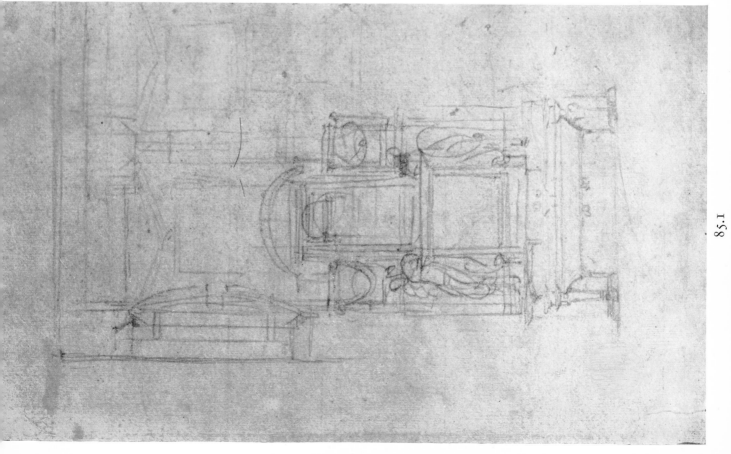

85.2

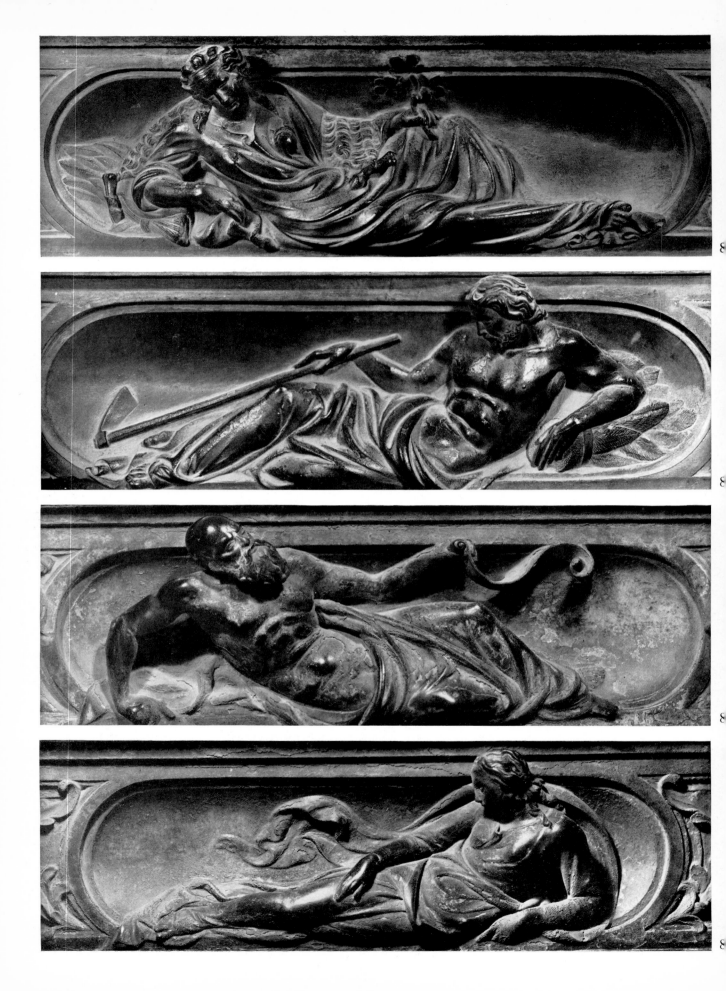

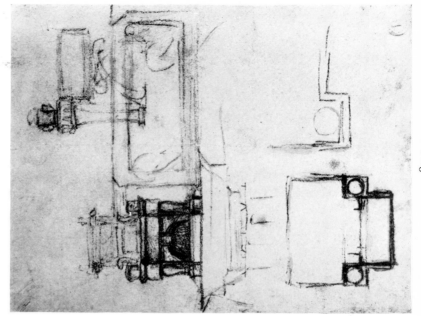

88.1

88.2

ROGGERIVS · MINERVET TVS · EQVÆS
GVÆLFOR · REIP · 7 · ARMOR · INSIGNIS
~ MORITVR · ANNO · M · CC · LXXX ·

FR · ARCHIEPVS · TVRRITANVS · 7 ·
EPVS · ARRETINVS · MERENTI ~
~ CONSANGVINE O ~
~ M · D · XXX ~

88.3

89.1

89.2

89.3

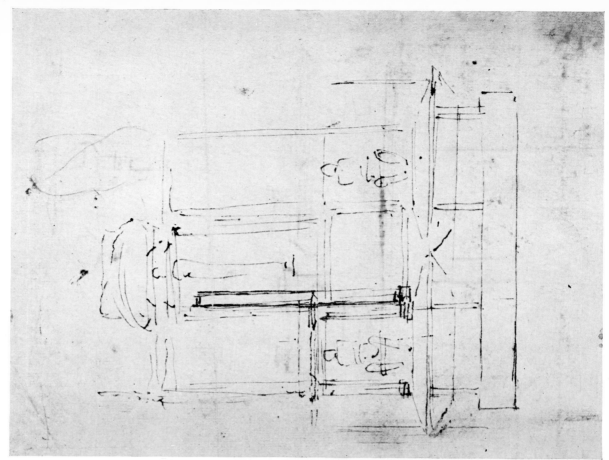

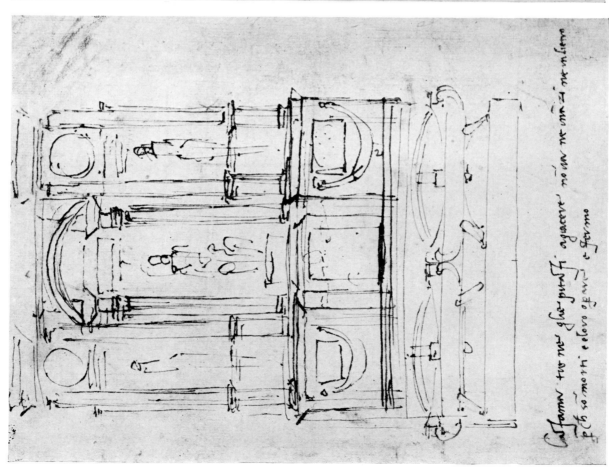

91

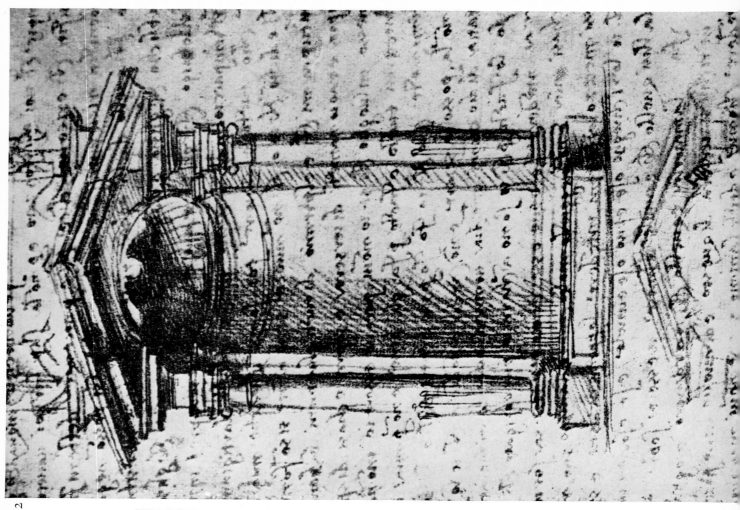

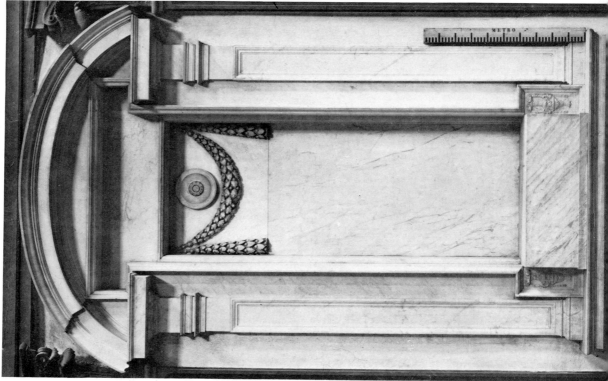

93

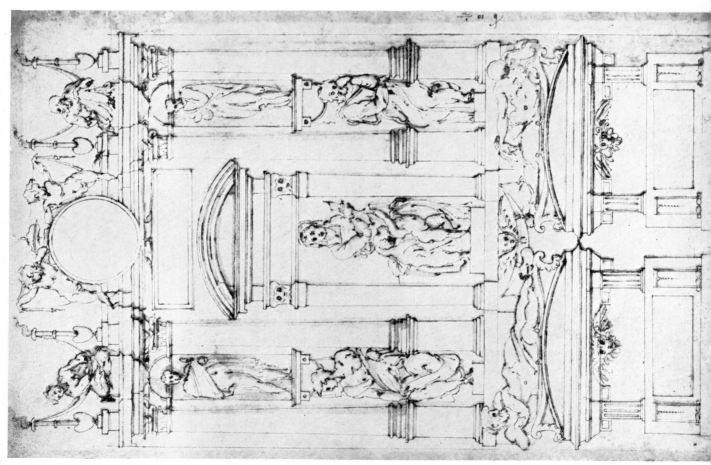

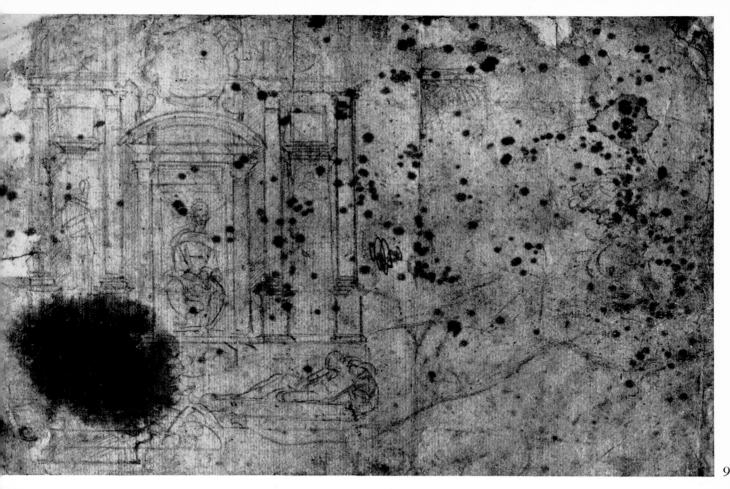

95.1

95.2

96.1

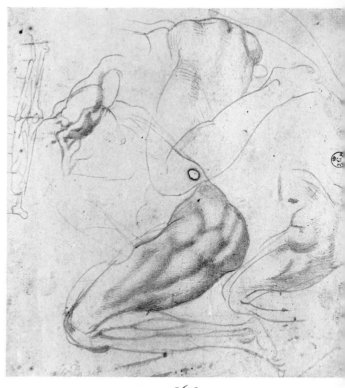

96.2

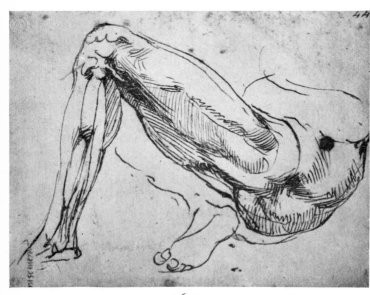

96.3

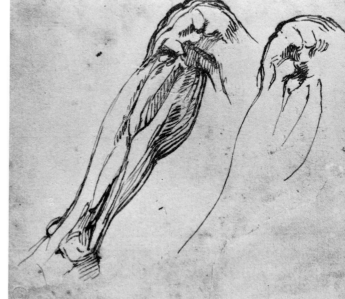

96.4

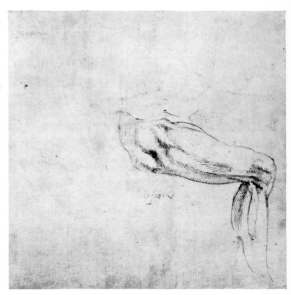

97.2

97.1

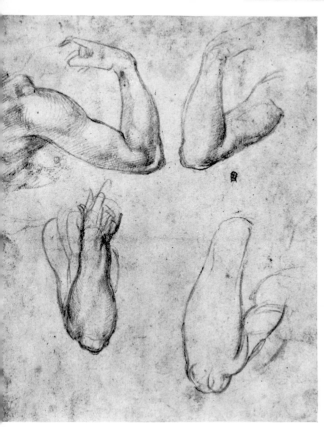

97.3

97.4

98.1

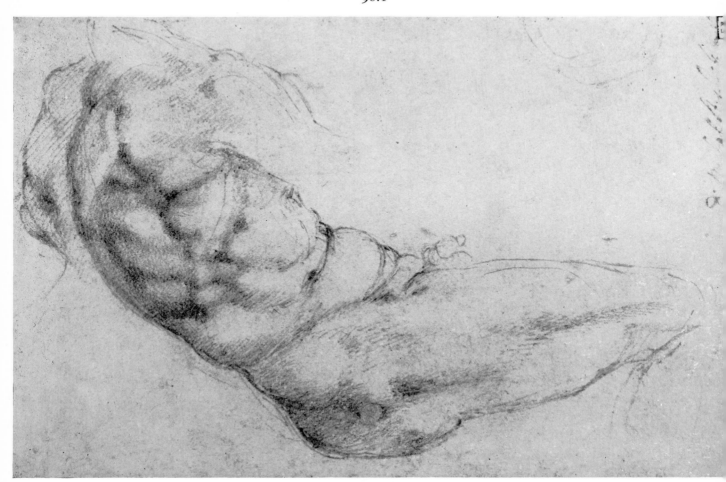

98.2

99.1

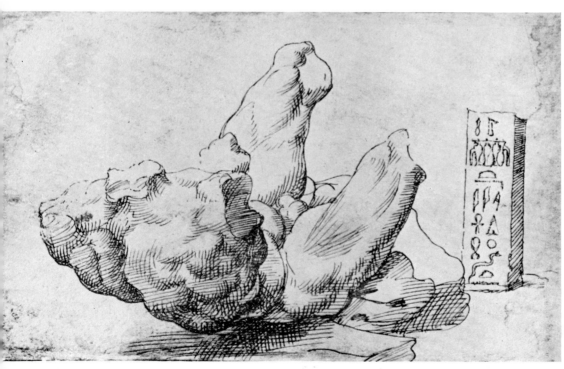

99.2

100

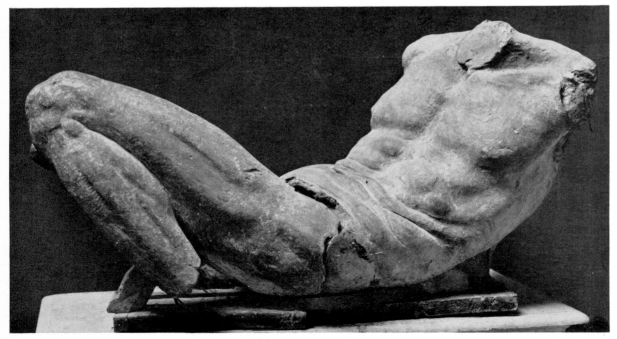

100.2

101.1

101.2

102.1

102.2

102.3

103.1

103.2

103.3

108.1

108.2

108.3

109.1

109.2

109.3

110.1

110.2

110.3

110.4

III.1

III.2

III.3

III.4

112.1

112.2

113.1

113.2

113.3

113.4

113.5

114.1   114.2

115.1

115.2

116.1

116.2

117.1

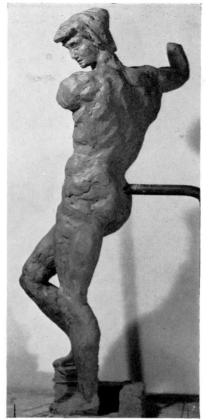

117.2

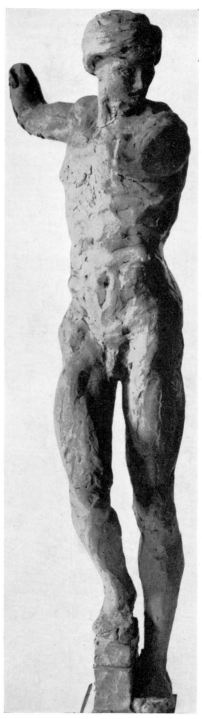

117.5

117.3

117.4

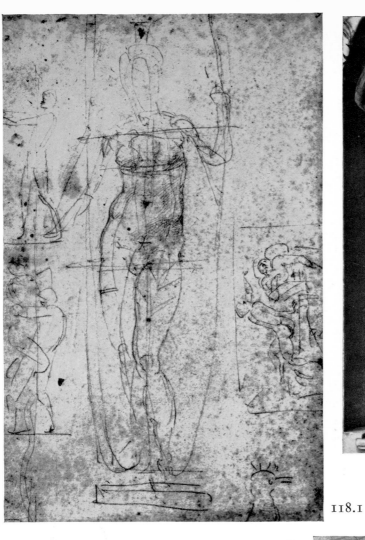

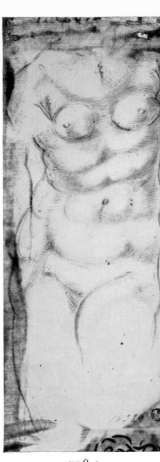

118.2

118.3

118.1

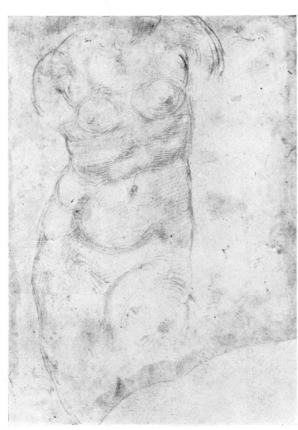

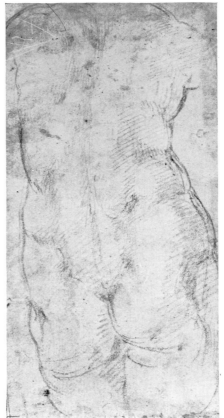

118.4

118.5

118.6

 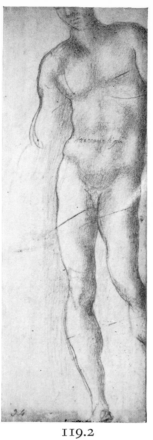

119.1   119.2

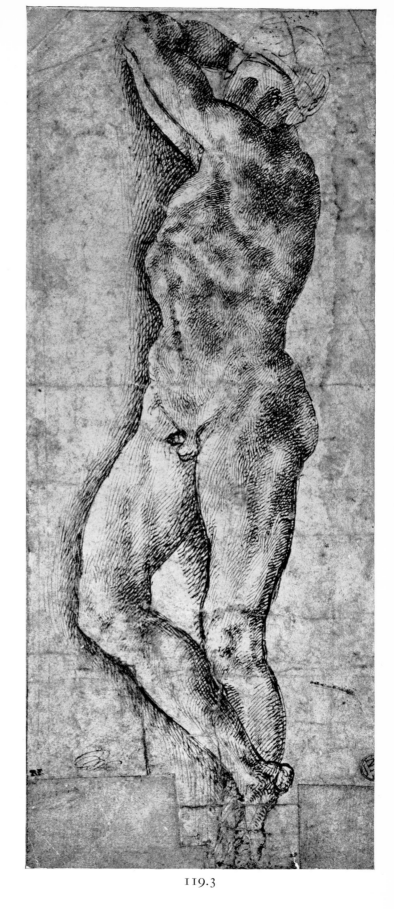

119.4

119.3

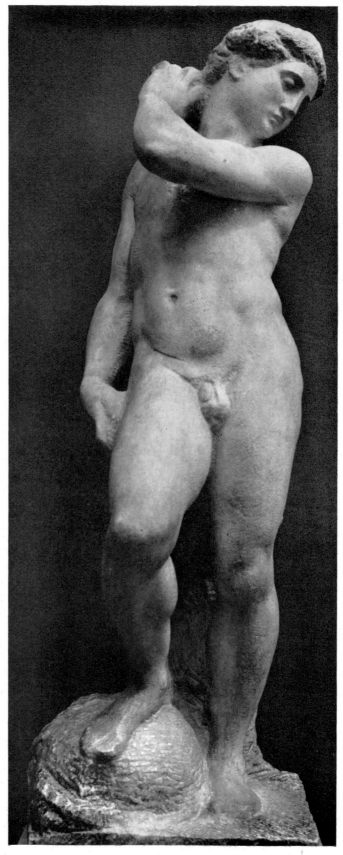

120

121.1

121.2

122.1

122.2

123.2

123.1

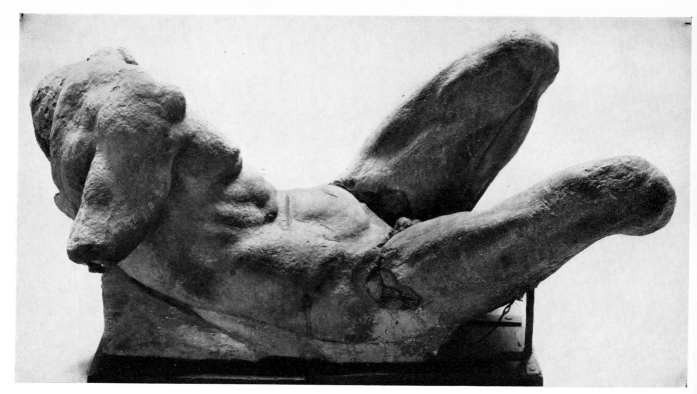

124.1

124.2

124.3

125.1

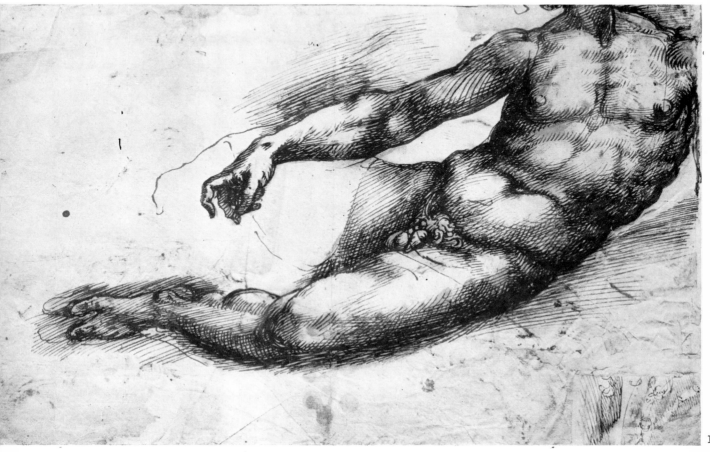

125.2

126.1

126.2

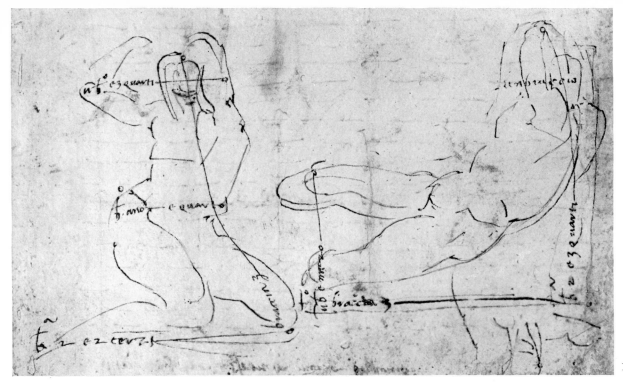

127.1

127.2

128.1

128.2

129.2

129.1

130.1

130.2

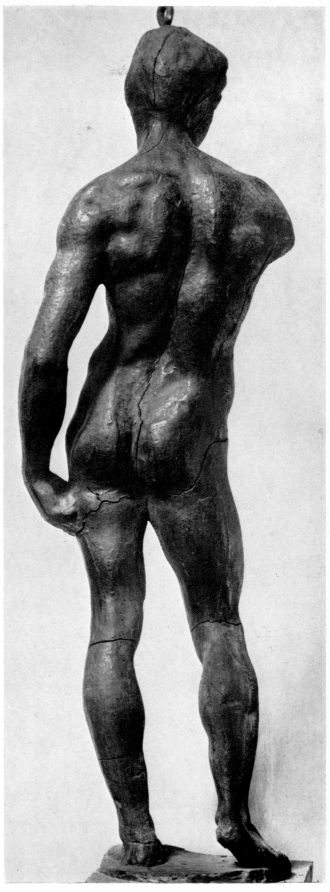

131.1   131.2

132.1

132.2

133.1

133.2

134.1

134.2

135.1

135.2

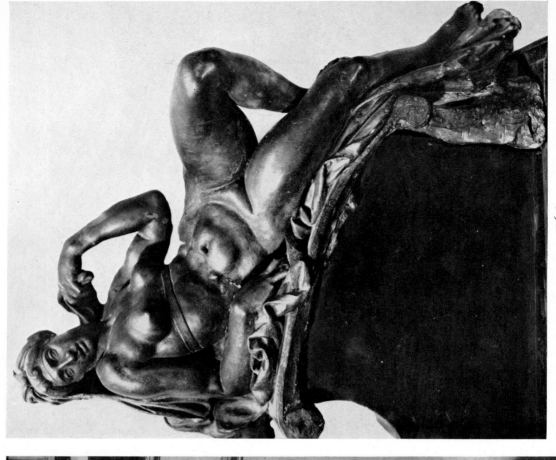

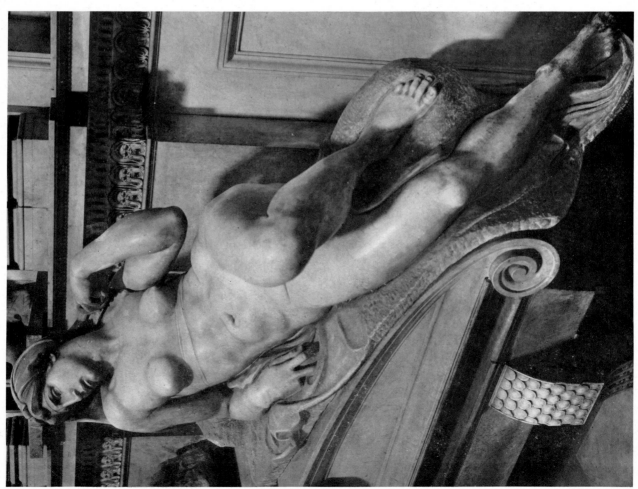

137.2

137.1

137.3

140.1

140.2

141.1

141.2

143

There is nothing that is meritorious but virtue and friendship, and, indeed, friendship itself is but a part of virtue.

ALEXANDER POPE

A Memoir of
the Author

MARTIN WEINBERGER left his work and his friends on September 6, 1965. This, his last book, was finished but for a few details and the Preface, which was to set forth its aim and scope. He had worked on the book for many years, and often, as among friends who have shared their ideas for a long time, we exchanged views on this or that detail, in a rather desultory fashion. He was aware of my lack of enthusiasm for his subject and never pressed the conversation so as to touch upon questions of principle or wider impact. When I saw him for the last time, I asked him why he had treated Michelangelo only as a sculptor, but, on that chilly morning on the beach at Forte de'Marmi, he was already too weak to tell me more than that the Preface was to give the reasons. This he was never allowed to write. The book will have to explain itself, and I trust that it will do so with clarity. And I shall write about him, recalling a lifelong close friendship.

It was in Italy that we met first and that I saw him for the last time. He had been appointed a fellow at the Kunsthistorisches Institut in Florence the same year as I, in 1926. Born in 1893 in Nuremberg, he was the older and had much more experience than I. Both of us had begun our careers in other fields. Weinberger had specialized in German painting and prints of the fifteenth and sixteenth centuries and in 1920 had taken his degree in Munich under Heinrich Wölfflin with a study on painting in fifteenth-century Nuremberg. He then entered a museum career at Munich, publishing books and articles on early German drawings and prints. He never lost his interest in this field, as shown by later publications, including a monograph on Wolf Huber. But he also had previous Italian experience. His article on Domenico Poggini (1925) was perhaps the first one to

407

open the field of Florentine sculpture of the sixteenth century, which later was to arouse my curiosity. For me, the younger, guided by Adolph Goldschmidt into the field of German medieval sculpture and a novice in Italy, Martin Weinberger's company was instructive and inspiring. Attracted by his intelligence, his literary, musical, and artistic interests and by his human warmth and kindness, I became closely attached to him. The resulting friendship was shared by his wife Edith, who was an ideal companion for him through his whole life and a true friend to his friends. As a Romance philologist and literary critic, she contributed much to our common stock of knowledge and to our talk, which ranged far and wide.

It is difficult to write briefly about lives so closely intertwined as ours; recollections of events lived together, of experiences shared, crowd up out of the past. There is a temptation to write more of our friendship than of him. I shall always remember with gratitude the help he lent me and with affection the gift of his friendship. And I shall always remember the time spent in his company, often hours of gaiety and pleasure but also of tragedy during the passage of history which darkened our lives.

We spent many years together in Florence, first those following our fellowship year, until Weinberger returned to Munich to resume his work in the museums, and others after 1933, when my friends were driven out of Germany. Our early association produced two articles; like the Goncourts, afterward we were never able to recognize each author's share.

During these years Weinberger mapped out the fields that were to occupy him during his whole life. He continued his interest in Italian Renaissance sculpture; the list of his works includes varied and original contributions in this field up to the end. These studies were to reach their fulfillment in the present book on Michelangelo. Unfortunately, he never finished a project long cherished and lovingly nourished at the same time—a history of Tuscan Gothic sculpture, with special emphasis on the Pisani and their circle. Many articles, reviews, and other contributions were written over the years in preparation for that work. Now they will remain a monumental fragment, a rich and valid contribution, that others must continue.

In Weinberger's work there is a gap after 1933 that marks the years after his emigration from Germany and during his pilgrimage through Italy, England, and the United States, until in 1937, the Institute of Fine Arts of New York University and our never to be forgotten friend, Walter W. S. Cook, offered him new scope for his talents. From then on there was a continuous flow of publications, made possible by his long experience in Italy. Weinberger taught at New York University until his retirement in 1958, well remembered by many as a scholar, as a teacher, and as a friend, and remained, emeritus, a valued member of the Institute until his death.

Martin Weinberger accepted the change that the conditions of the world wrought in his life with a remarkable equanimity, which, however, was not based on indifference. During the long time of transition, his mind continued to work constructively. I was with him in periods of heavy stress—in 1933, when he came to Italy; on his first Atlantic crossing, when he went toward an uncertain future; on a visit to Chicago during his first orientation trip through the United States—and I remember these occasions vividly. His intellectual faculties were unimpaired by these trials; his warm humanity was even enhanced. His optimism—not a thoughtless one—and his faith in man were eventually justified by the generosity of his colleagues in the United States, without whose help my friend, like so many others, would have been doomed.

Men who have mastered such difficult circumstances are not simple. Any honest and moral soul under such conditions is torn in many directions. Bitterness haunts them. They can become neighbors to despair, and it is a sign of great strength if they succeed in preserving their equilibrium.

Martin Weinberger was a very complex person. His gifts were many: his interests embraced everything that was human; his artistic tastes were accompanied by a warm heart capable of the most loyal friendship, by a bizarre sense of humor which made him a welcome partner in every kind of musical and literary parlor game, by an intellectual honesty and purity which occasionally must have made him appear, to those who did not know him well, brusque or crusty. He attracted friends for a lifetime, among them the writer of these lines, but occasionally he also antagonized people who probably failed to understand him and whom he did not care to reconcile.

It may have been the very complexity of his mind that enabled him to survive the shock of 1933 with almost no damage to his personality. His many experiences helped him to achieve that intellectual discrimination and tact which are the essence of freedom of mind. The test lay in this: he grew up in Germany; since his boyhood he was attached to the art of his native city, Nuremberg. He served in World War I and was wounded, and his right arm remained crippled. I have known few victims of the Nazi persecution who bore an undeserved fate with such inner dignity and fair-minded wisdom. He never lost his love for the art of his country of origin.

I believe that Martin Weinberger would have liked the words of Alexander Pope that I have set at the beginning of these pages. They characterize him, particularly in their exclusiveness, which admits of no worldly ambition, vanity, lust for power, greed, or envy, in all of which he was so conspicuously lacking. And they assume that friendship is a natural manifestation of such virtue as his.

I have dwelt on the aspects of Martin Weinberger's life and on the qualities that were

familiar perhaps only to his intimates. His scholarly work and its significance are on record; the value of his writings will be appreciated by all who use them. They do remain. To the friend himself we had to bid farewell. I hope that the faint image that I have drawn of him in these pages may help to preserve his memory.

ULRICH MIDDELDORF

Works by
Martin Weinberger

Books

Nürnberger Malerei an der Wende zur Renaissance und die Anfänge der Dürerschule. Strasbourg, I. H. E. Heitz, 1921.

Deutsche Rokokozeichnungen. Munich, Delphin Verlag, 1923.

Albrecht Dürer. Munich, Delphin Verlag, 1924.

Die Formschnitte des Katharinenklosters zu Nürnberg. Munich, Verlag der Münchner Drucke, 1925.

Jakob Ruysdael. Munich, Delphin Verlag, 1925.

Wolfgang Huber. Leipzig, Insel Verlag, 1930

The George Gray Barnard Collection. New York, 1941.

Articles

Zur Geschichte der Oberrheinischen Malerei in 15. Jahrhundert, *Münchner Jahrbuch der Bildenden Kunst*, 1923.

Über die Herkunst des Meisters LCZ. *In* Festschrift für Heinrich Wölfflin, Munich, 1924.

Ein Altar vom Meister des Cadolzburger Altars, *Cicerone*, 1925.

Marmorskulpturen von Domenico Poggini, *Zeitschrift für Bildenden Kunst*, 1925.

Der Meister der Biberacher Sippe, *Münchner Jahrbuch der Bildenden Kunst*, 1926.

Unbeachtete Werke der Brüder Rossellino (in collaboration with U. Middeldorf), *Münchner Jahrbuch der Bildenden Kunst*, 1928.

Französische Madonnen des frühen 14. Jahrhunderts in Toscana (in collaboration with U. Middeldorf), *Pantheon*, 1928.

Zu Dürers Lehr- und Wanderjahren, *Münchner Jahrbuch der Bildenden Kunst*, 1929.

Die Ausstellung kirchlicher Kunstschätze in München, *Zeitschrift für Bildenden Kunst*, 1930.

Die Erlanger Handzeichnungssammlung in München, *Cicerone*, 1930.

Bildnisbüsten von Guido Mazzoni, *Pantheon*, 1930.

Sammlung Schloss Rohoncz II: Plastik und Kunstgewerbe, *Cicerone*, 1930.

Eine Madonna von Giovanni Pisano, *Jahrbuch der Preussischen Kunstsammlungen*, 1930.

Sperandio und die Frage der Francia Skulpturen, *Münchner Jahrbuch der Bildenden Kunst*, 1930.

Kleine Beiträge zur Lokalisierung früher Holzschnitte, *Mitteilungen der Gesellschaft für Vervielfältigende Kunst*, 1930.

Die Madonna am Nordportal von Notre Dame, *Zeitschrift für Bildende Kunst*, 1930.

Bronze Statuettes by Giovanni Caccini, *Burlington Magazine*, 1931.

Ausstellung Nürnberger Malerei 1350–1450, *Bamberger Blätter für fränkische Kunst und Geschichte*, VIII (1931).

Ein Augsburger Pestblatt, *Beitrage zur Forschung, Studien aus dem Antiquariat Jacques Rosenthal*, 1932.

Über einige Jugendwerke von Hans Sebald Beham und Verwandtes, *Mitteilungen der Gesellschaft für vervielfältigende Kunst*, 1932.

Zu Cranachs Jugendentwicklung, *Zeitschrift für Kunstgeschichte*, 1933.

The Master of S. Giovanni, *Burlington Magazine*, 1937.

Giovanni Pisano: (1) A New Discovery. (2) Remarks on the Technique of the Master's Workshop, *Burlington Magazine*, 1937.

Nino Pisano, *Art Bulletin*, 1937.

'New' Rembrandts, *Magazine of Art*, XXX (1937).

13th Century Frescoes at Montepiano, *Art in America*, 1939.

A Bronze Bust by Hans Multscher, *Art Bulletin*, 1940.

Silkweaves of Lucca and Venice in Contemporary Painting and Sculpture, *Bulletin of the Needle and Bobbin Club*, 1941.

The First Façade of the Cathedral of Florence, *Journal of the Warburg and Courtauld Institutes*, LV (1941).

A Portrait Bust by Pietro Torregiani, *The Compleat Collector*, 1944.

A Document of Early Medieval Architecture, *The Compleat Collector*, 1944.

A Dutch Painting (by P. van Noort), *The Compleat Collector*, 1944.

A Gothic Model by the School of Jacques Morel, *Bulletin of the Walters Art Gallery*, 1945.

The Bust of Antonio Galli in the Frick Collection, *Gazette des Beaux-Arts*, 1945.

A Sixteenth Century Restorer, *Art Bulletin*, 1945.

A High Renaissance Madonna (by Jacone), *The Compleat Collector*, 1945.

An Italian Reliquary Bust of the Early 15th Century, *The Compleat Collector*, 1945.

A. Boucher's 'À la Terre,' *The Compleat Collector*, 1945.

Recumbent Tomb Statue of a Knight in the Philadelphia Museum, *Art Quarterly*, 1945.

Three Paintings by Masters of the School of Utrecht, *The Compleat Collector*, 1945.

Original and Copy, *The Compleat Collector*, 1945.

A Newly Discovered Portrait by Antoine Vestier, *The Compleat Collector*, 1945.

An Early Woodcut of the Man of Sorrows at the Art Institute, Chicago, *Gazette des Beaux-Arts*, 1945.

A French Model of the 15th Century, *Journal of the Walters Art Gallery*, 1946.

Notes on Maitre Michiel, *Burlington Magazine*, 1948.

Rembrandt's Portrait of Constantijn a Renesse, *Gazette des Beaux-Arts*, 1948.

A Renaissance Restorer (Valerio Cioli), *Art Bulletin*, 1949.

A Bronze Bust in the Frick Collection, *Gazette des Beaux-Arts*, 1951.

A Bronze Statuette in the Frick Collection and Its Connection with Michelangelo, *Gazette des Beaux-Arts*, Tietze Festschrift, 1952.

Nicola Pisano and the Tradition of Pisan pulpits, *Gazette des Beaux-Arts*, 1959.

Remarks on the Role of French Models within the Evolution of Gothic Tuscan Sculpture. International Congress of the History of Art. Acts. Studies in Western Art, I, Princeton University Press, 1963.

The Chair of Dagobert, *Essays in Memory of Karl Lehmann* (published by *Marsyas*), 1964.

Arnolfo und die Ehrenstatue Karls von Anjou. *In* Studien zur Geschichte der europäischen Plastik, Festschrift für Theodor Müller, Munich, 1965.

Bemerkung zu einer Michelangelo Zeichnung. *In* Festschrift für Ulrich Middeldorf, 1966 [posthumously published].

Selected Reviews

Planiscig, Leo: Piccoli bronzi Italiani, *Zeitschrift für Bildende Kunst*, 1931.

Rackham, Bernard: Victoria and Albert Museum Catalogue of Italian Majolica, *Art Bulletin*, 1942.

Tolnay, Charles de: The Youth of Michelangelo (Princeton, 1943), *Art Bulletin*, 1945.

Gantner, Joseph: Romanische Plastik, *Art Bulletin*, 1949.

Antal, Frederick: Florentine Painting and Its Social Background, *College Art Journal*, X (1951), 199–202.

Carli, Enzo: La scultura del Duomo di Orvieto, *Art Bulletin*, 1952.

Toesca, Ilaria: Andrea and Nino Pisano, *Art Bulletin*, 1953.

Dupont, Jacques, and Cesare Gnudi: Gothic Painting, *Saturday Review*, 1955.

Weihrauch, Hans: Die Bildwerke in Bronze im Bayrischen Nationalmuseum (Munich, 1956), *Art Bulletin*, 1958.

Müller, Th., and A. Feulner: Geschichte der deutschen Plastik, 1953, *Erasmus*, 1956.

Matejek-Pešina: Gotische Malerei in Böhmen (Prague, 1955), *Erasmus*, 1958.

Comte de Salverte: Les ébénistes du 18me siècle, *Erasmus*, 1958.

INDEXES

Index of Works by Michelangelo

Academy Slaves, *see* Slaves, for Tomb of Julius II; *Atlas*; *Awakening Captive*; *Bearded Captive*; *Youthful Captive*

Active Life, see Guiliano; Leah

Allegories, see *Leah*; *Rachel*; *Times of Day*

Angel, shrine of St. Dominic, Bologna, Plate *14.2*, 52–53; and Niccolò dell'Arca *Angel*, Plate *14*, 52; ornament, 66*n*19; and head of *David*, 90

Apollo (*David-Apollo*), Plates *120*, *121*, 343, 345–51; drawings, 345–47; dating, 347, 350; ownership, 348; drawing by Salviati, 349–50; and Medici Chapel statues, 350–51; and statuette by Danti, 360

Apostles (projected), for Cathedral of Florence, 96–98; study, Plate *31.1* 98; commission taken from Michelangelo, 125. *See also St. Matthew*

Atlas, for Tomb of Julius II, Plate *60.2*, 169, 200*n*12; pose and projected setting, 213–17; side view, Plate *62.1*, 213, 216; dating, 217; dimensions, 217*n*53; in Plan of *1532*, 260, 265; style, 325; and statues of Medici Chapel, 325

Awakening Captive, for Tomb of Julius II, Plate *61.1*, 168; pose and projected setting, 212, 213, 216; side view, Plate *62.2*, 216; in Plan of *1532*, 260, 265

Bacchus, Plates *16*, *17*, *18*, 60–68; drawing by Heemskerck, Plate *19.2*, 63; face, Plate *17*, 64, 65, 124; faun, 67, 120; and Victory groups, 266; statuettes by Danti, 360

Barbazza, Bartolomeo, tomb, 229

Bathing Soldiers, see Battle of Cascina

Battle of Cascina, cartoon, 98–99, 105–7, 109, 122, 125; drawings, Plates *31.1*, *31.2*, *41.1*, *42.1*, *43.1*, *45.2*, 105–7; grisaille copy by Aristotile da Sangallo, Plate *42.2*, 106, 107

Battle of Centaurs, Plate *10*, 5, 38–45, 65, 123, 126, 384; and Bertoldo, Plate *5*, 42

Bearded Captive, for Tomb of Julius II, Plate *61.2*, 167, 210–11, 213, 216, 259–60; and *Laocoön*, 175; models, 210–11; side view, Plate *62.2*, 212; dimensions, 217*n*53; in plan of *1532*, 265

Bearded Captive, clay model (attributed), Plate *63.1*, 211*n*48

Bruges *Madonna, see Madonna*, Bruges

Brutus, Plate *112.1*, 330, 331, 398

Christ, Santa Maria sopra Minerva, Plate *58*, 176, 185, 200–9; first version, 201; marble, 201; site, 201, 205, 209; and Louvre Slaves, 202, 203; drawings, Plates *59.2*, *59.3*, 203–4; diagonal view, Plate *59.1*, 203–5; copies, 204; damage by assistant, 206, 207*n*37; iconography, 207–9; style, 325; and *Apollo*, 350

Contemplative Life, see Lorenzo; Rachel

Crouching Boy, Plate *144*, 397–98

Crucifixion of St. Peter, Pauline Chapel, 278, 279*n*28

Cupid, 59–60

David, Plate *24*, 50, 77–92, 107, 119; and antique, 74, 89–90; work of Agostino on block, 78–85; Plate *26.2*, 81–82, 87; composition, 81–88; back view, *David*, Plate *25.3*, 84*n*14; and late *quattrocento*, 88–92; and Donatello *David*, Plate *23.2*, 88; and Federighi *Bacchus*, Plate *25.4*, 89; and *Pietà*, 89; site, 90–91; and *St. Proculus*, 89; criticism by Leonardo and Raphael, 91–92; criticism by Michelangelo, 92, 117, 247; and Sansovino *St. James*, 125; and group for the Piazza, 246–50; and head of *Giuliano*, Plate *110.3*, 330; and *Apollo*, 348; alleged models, 360, 361

David, bronze (lost), 87, 96–97; reconstructions, Plates *30.2*, *30.3*, 96; stance, 116

David-Apollo, see *Apollo*

Dawn, Medici Chapel, Plate *103.1*, 317–20; and statues for Tomb of Julius II, 265; and Ghiberti's *Eve*, 311; rear view, Plate *103.2*, 319; head, Plate *108.3*, 322; profile, Plate *109.2*, 322; and drawing of Phaeton, 326; as ideal type, 329; and cartouche style, 335*n*12; clay model, 357; setting, Plate *136.1*, 357, 365–67; and River Gods, 358; Tribolo copy, Plate *136.2*, 361, 365, 366; damage, 362; iconography, 390–91, 393*n*13

Day, Medici Chapel, Plate *101.1*, 317–20; drawings, Plates *84.1*, *97.1*, *98.1*, 310, 312–14; and Belvedere torso and River God, 319; rear view, Plate *102.2*, 319; dating, 323; and *Atlas*, 325; and scale of sarcophagus, 361; marble block, 362; Plate *135.1*, 362–64, 393*n*13; setting, in original plan, Tribolo copy, Plate *135.2*, 364; setting, on sarcophagus, 364–65; damage, 364

Delphic Sibyl, Plate *36*, 100, 103, 113, 124, 203

Dominic, St., shrine at Bologna, 48–53, 149*n*21. *See also* *Angel*; *St. Petronius*; *St. Proculus*

Doni *Madonna*, see *Madonna*, Doni

Drawings: after Giotto's *Ascension of St. John*, Plate *1.2*, 17–18; of kneeling figure, Plate *2.3*, 18–25; of three standing figures, Plates *2.1*, *2.3*, 18–25; after Masaccio's *Tribute Money*, Plate *3.3*, 17–18, 26–27; man in long cloak, Plate *15.2*, 50, 53–55; of various figures, Plate *19.1*, 66–67, 123*n*47; for bronze *David*, Plate *30.1*, 86–88, 96, 124; anatomical studies, Plates *26.1*, *27*, *30.1*, 87, 104, 123; St. Anne, the Virgin, and Child, Plate *40.2*, 87, 104; *David*, after Donatello, 97*n*9; for *Battle of Cascina*, Plate *31.1*, 98–99, 116, 125; architectural studies, Plate *31.2*, 98, 99; for a Madonna and Child, Plate *32.1*, 103–4; head of Doni *Madonna*, Plate *32.2*, 103; St. Anne and the Virgin, Plate *40.1*, 104, 112, 120, 123; of children, Plate *41.2*, 105; anatomical studies, *Battle of Cascina*, and children, Plates *42.1*, *43.1*, 106, 107; of beckoning youth, Plate *41.1*, 107, 121; of Madonnas, Plate *48.2*, 113*n*32;

putto, Plate *45.1*, 116, 117, 120*n*46, 167; variant of *David*, Plate *45.3*, 117, 121; study of arm, Plates *44.2*, *45.2*, 117, 124*n*48; of Apostle, Plate *43.3*, 106–7, 117*n*40; Mercury-Apollo, Plate *44.1*, 117–21, 203*n*26; for Bruges *Madonna*, 121; Apollonian youth, Plate *44.2*, 121, 124*n*48; for *Christ* of the Minerva, Plates *59.2*, *59.3*, 203; architectural, for San Silvestro in Capite (Plate *66.2*), 228–30; two struggling figures, Plate *69.2*, 238, 242–43; for *Hercules and Antaeus*, Plate *68*, 240, 314, 341*n*8, 344; Ganymede, 250; for *Last Judgment*, Plate *76.3*, 261*n*27, 264, 303; *Virgin Annunciate*, Plate *77.1*, 79, 278; Eridanus, 326, 358, 359; Phaeton, 326, 358; alleged portraits, 330*n*2; Sibyl or Prophet, Plate *123.1*, 340–41; dragon, Plate *122.1*, 341–42; dragon, copy, Plate *122.2*, 342*n*9, 349, head of satyr, Plate *132.2*, 341*n*8; Venus, Plates *118.4*, *118.5*, 344; Cupid and Psyche, 344; Samson and Delilah, 353*n*5; *Children's Bacchanal*, 387; *Bersaglio degli dei*, 387. *See also* Julius II, tomb; Medici Chapel

Dying Slave, Plate *52.2*, 166, 167, 211; and head of ape, 145–46, 169; dimensions, 169; bridge between chest and elbow, Plate *54.1*, 170; and *Ignudi*, 171; and *Laocoön*, 171–72, 175; and *Dead Niobid*, 172; projected setting, 187; finish, 261*n*26; and *carcere terreno*, 382, 384

Earth (projected for Medici Chapel): small model, Plates *114*, *115*, 263–64, 339–40; marble block, 309; iconography, 338, 344–45, 347–48, 395–96; copies, 343*n*11; and Cellini *Minerva*, 344; drawings, Plates *118.1*, *118.4*, *118.5*, 344; projected setting, Plate *138*, 370

'Earth' (*Cybele*), in *1505* plan for Tomb of Julius II, 133

Erythrean Sibyl, 25

Evening, Plate *102.1*, 317–20; and *Dawn*, 319–20; head, 324–25; and River Gods, 326, 358; clay model, 357; Tribolo copy, Plate *133.2*, 361, 365; damage, 362; setting, 365–66; iconography, 393*n*13

Farnese Palace, 368, 371

Faun, head, 4

Giovannino (lost *Young St. John*), 56, 58

Giuliano, Medici Chapel, Plate *105*, 320–24; head, Plate *111.2*, 265, 326, 330; iconography, 266, 332–36, 397; drawings, Plates *87.1*, *97.4*, 314–15, 323, 345*n*15; dating, 321; setting, Plate *107*, 321; profile, Plate *110.3*, 322; rear view, Plate *113.2*, 322–23; baton, 336; and Montorsoli *Apollo*, Plate *112.2*, 345*n*15; lost model, 345*n*15; and *Madonna*, Plate *93*, 372

Group for the Piazza (projected), 225, 237–50, 325; work of Bandinelli, 237–39, 248–49; marble block, 242, 248–49; wax model (*Hercules and Antaeus*), 240; *Hercules and Antaeus*, drawings, Plate *68*, 240, 314; *Samson and Two Philistines*, bronze casts from wax model, Plate *70*, 204, 241–42; and clay model of two fighting men, Plates *73, 75*, 245–49; height, 249–50; and drawing of Ganymede, 250

Heaven (projected for Medici Chapel): lost model, 263–64, 339, 341–44; marble block, 309; iconography, 338, 339, 345; pose, 340; drawing after model, Plate *116*, 341–42; reconstruction, Plates *117.1, 117.2, 117.5*, 341; and Cellini's *Mercury*, Plate *117.3*, 343; copy as Mercury, Plate *117.4*, 344; and *Apollo*, 350–51; projected setting, Plate *138*, 370

'Heaven' (*Cielo*), in *1505* plan for Tomb of Julius II, 132–33, 136

Hercules (lost), 43–47; as shown in prints, Plates *11.1, 11.2*, 45–46; and antique works, 47; and Bertoldo, 47

Hercules and Antaeus (lost wax model), 240, 268, 325; drawing, Plate *68*, 240, 314

Hercules and Cacus, *see* Group for the Piazza; Victory group, male

Ignudi, Sistine ceiling, and *Rebellious Slave*, Plate *53.1*, 171

Julius II ('Pope of Bologna'), bronze (destroyed), 122, 126, 223

Julius II, statue on his tomb, 135–36; setting, 148–49, 275–76; block, 180; in *1516* plan, 194, 195; profile drawing, Plate *67.4*, 195; work of Tommaso Boscoli, 273

Julius II, Tomb of, Plates *80, 81.2*, 129–234, 253–80; iconography, 6, 130–32, 139, 144, 146, 149, 151*n*23, 277, 382, 384; and Sistine ceiling, 126; form of sarcophagus, 135–36; and Belvedere sarcophagus, Plate *50.3*, 137–38; and Rovere family, 129, 221–27, 231–34, 253–57, 270, 294; and tomb of Charles, Duke of Orléans, 141–42; marble, 150, 153, 177–80; and Julius II, 150–52, 156–57; and Medici Popes, 189–91, 255–56, 269; scale, 217; assistants to Michelangelo, 270–73; and Paul III, 272; completion, 273; and Rossellino, 369

architecture: plan of *1505*, 129–52; herm busts, 131–32, 145, 179, 193, 218*n*55, 274; dimensions, 131–34, 137–39, 153, 155–58, 161, 163–64, 197; chamber, 133, 135; reconstructions, 134, 140, 147, 154–55, 162–63, 192, 214, 260; decoration, 138–39, 144–45,

153–56, 196, 273*n*22; as free-standing monument, 149; as *moles Julii*, 150, 152; first plan of *1513*, 153–59; models, 157, 161–63, 190; enlarged plan of *1513*, 160–68; façade, Plate *67.1*, 186; as wall tomb, 186, 224, 225, 227, 257; plan of *1516*, Plate *67.1*, 189–97; as *cappelletta*, 193–94, 196; High Renaissance style, 196; plan of *1519*, Plate *66.1*, 198–219, 230; *1516* and *1519* plans compared, 198–219; plan of *1526*, 220–34, 256–57; plan of *1532*, 232–33, 253–61, 269; and figures, 274–76, 370

drawings: for Slave, Plate *45.2*, 117, 124*n*48; architectural, plan of *1516*, Plates *67.1, 67.2*, 130, 186, 193*n*10, 196–97, 217*n*52; for six Slaves, Plate *49*, 145, 166–70, 185, 188, 212; of Slave, Plate *53.2*, 167, 185; profile of Pope, Plate *67.4*, 195; architectural (*1518*?), Plate *66.3*, 227–28, 231; —, plan of *1519*, Plate *66.1*, 227–28, 230–31; for Victory group, Plate *77.2*, 261*n*27

statues: clay models, 130, 211; number, 135, 153–56, 181–82, 191–93, 199–200, 257–59; by assistants, 211, 270–73. *See also* Slaves; *individual works*

Last Judgment, 208*n*42, 261, 270, 330, 382

Laurentian Library, 4*n*4, 146, 186, 222, 335, 344; and Tomb of Julius II, 190; and Medici Chapel, Plate *142*, 299–300; pavement, 344; Ricetto, 371, 404

Leah, Plate *79*, 132, 175, 219; as *Active Life*, 258, 266, 272; final setting, 276; iconography, 277; composition, 278–80; and portraiture, 329, 331

Leda and the Swan (lost painting), study, 313

Lorenzo, Medici Chapel, Plate *104*, 327–38; drawings, Plates *95.2, 97.2*, 304*n*37, 314–15, 336; composition, 320–22; dating, 321; rear view, Plate *113.1*, 322; head, Plate *111.4*, 322; reconstruction of tomb, with *Day* and *Night*, Plate *139*, 335; iconography, 332–36; as *Il Pensieroso*, 334–36; and niche figures, 347, 393, 396; and *Madonna*, 372

Louvre Slaves, *see* Slaves, for Tomb of Julius II; *Dying Slave*; *Rebellious Slave*

Madonna, Bruges, Plates *37.2, 48.1*, 109–17, 122; profile, Plate *39.3*, 95; and Signorelli *Madonna*, 103; dimensions, 110; composition, 110, 112, 116, 119; perspective, 110, 113; studies, Plates *42.1, 48.2*, 110, 113*n*32, 114, 116, 120; drapery, 111; and Donatello's *Judith*, 111–12; and *Pietà*, 111–14; and *Delphic Sibyl*, 113; dating, 113–15, 117; and Pitti *Madonna*, 122; and *St. Matthew*, 122; and Doni *Madonna*, 123; and *Christ* of Minerva, 203

Madonna, Doni, Plate *33*, 24, 97, 100–5; and *Delphic Sibyl*, 100, 103, 113; dating, 100, 104, 105; and *David*, 100, 105; and Taddei *Madonna*, 100, 105; composition, 100–2, 105, 203; frame, 101; and Signorelli, 101, 102; and Leonardo's St. Anne, 101, 105; color, 102–3; criticism, 102–3; drawing for head, Plate *32.2*, 103; and *Young St. John*, 103–4; and Bruges *Madonna*, 123; arm, 403–4

Madonna, Medici Chapel, Plate *82*, 217, 290; setting, Plates *91, 93*, 290, 303; dimensions, 301, 308; composition, 321–23; head, Plate *108.2*, 322; profile, Plate *109.1*, 322; and *Atlas*, 325; dating, 326; copy, 342*n*9; model, 355; iconography, 371, 396

Madonna, Pitti, Plate *35*, 95; and Doni *Madonna*, 100; and St. Anne drawing, 104; dating, 109, 114; and Donatello's *Judith*, 111–12, 125; head, Plate *39.2*, 111–13, 122; and Bruges *Madonna*, 122; surface treatment, 122; and *St. Matthew*, 123; mood, 124

Madonna, Taddei, Plate *34*, 96, 98; and *quattrocento*, 100; and Doni *Madonna*, 100, 105; and *David*, 105; dating, 105, 108, 114; figure of St. John in, Plates *41.2, 43.1*, 107–9; and Raphael, 108–9, 115; unfinished state, 108, 125

Madonna of the Stairs, Plate *9*, 30–38; and Donatello's *Madonna in the Clouds*, 31, 33, 35–36; and Desiderio's *Madonna and Child*, 31–32; composition, 32–34; and antiquity, 33–34; and Bertoldo, 34–35; modeling, 36; discovery, 38

Medici Chapel, Plates *82, 93, 143*, 130, 283–372, 386–98; iconography, 6, 266, 268, 312, 338, 369–70, 386–99; and Sistine ceiling, 126; and Tomb of Julius II, 190, 368; early plans, 191, 220, 221, 363; models, 287*n*11, 295–96, 327; and wall tombs, 288*n*14, 289–90, 368–69; marble, 292, 293, 295, 299–309; and Clement VII, 292–94, 306–7; assistants to Michelangelo, 297, 299 302, 305, 307*n*52, 316*n*1, 336, 337, 339, 356, 361; plan of *1524*, 299, 301, 302, 308; style and interpretation in, 386–98

  architecture: as free-standing monument, 130, 135*n*11, 141, 286, 288*n*14, 368; setting of tombs, 285*n*7; marble, 299–309; tabernacles, Plates *90.1, 92.2, 93*, 300–1, 303; vault, Plate *82*, 305; lantern, 305; of ducal monuments, 320–21, 368–69, 393–94; dimensions, 356; scale, 368–69, 371*n*3; and statues, 368–72, 386, 393; and dome of St. Peter's, 371; and Laurentian Library, *Ricetto*, Plate *142*, 371*n*3; doors, 372

  decoration: trophy and swags, Plate *87.1*, 148*n*21, 149–50; half-balusters, 165*n*4, 295–96; frieze of masks, Plate *89.3*, 297; serpents, 298; trophy, unfinished, Plate *88.2*, 298; trophy, and work of Cosini,

Plate *88.1*, 298; candlestick, Plate *89.2*, 298; scrolls, 304

  drawings: architectural, Plates *83, 85, 87, 90, 92.2, 94, 95*, 284–91, 297, 299–305, 363, 336, 390–94; of thrones, Plate *87.2*, 297, 304; of tabernacle, Plate *92.2*, 300, 302; figure (attributed), Plate *76.3*, 303; niche figure, nude woman, 309; for main statues, 310–15, 390–93, 397; arm of *Night*, Plate *97.3*, 313, 363; for *Day*, Plates *97.1, 98.1*, 312–14; for *Night* or *Leda*, Plate *96.3*, 313–14, 353; for *Night* or *Giuliano*, Plate *97.4*, 313–15, 323, 356; various studies and owl of *Night*, Plate *68.2*, 314; leg of *Night*, Plates *96.1, 96.2*, 314; 'ground plan' for *River God*, Plate *127.1*, 314, 356–59; leg of *Lorenzo*, Plate *97.2*, 315, 353; *Minerva*, Plate *118.1*, 344; for *Night* (?), Plate *96.4*, 353; for *River God*, Plate *125.2*, 353–54

  statues: marble 292–94; models, 305–6, 309, 355–56, 365; dimensions, 308; evolution, 314–15; work on, to *1524*, 316; style, 316–26; dating, 317, 321–23, 327; work on, to *1526*, 323–24; casts, 324*n*10; work on, to *1531*, 325; work by Michelangelo on, 352, 355, 358; and sarcophagus lids, 365; and architecture, 368–72, 386, 393; relationship to each other, 370–72. *See also individual works*

  wall tombs: setting, 285*n*7, 337–38; sarcophagi, Plate *85.1*, 289*n*15, 311, 361–67; dimensions of statues, 301, 319; work in *1524*, 305–9; niche figures, 309, 338–47, 370–71, *see also Heaven and Earth*; contrasted, 320, 330–31, 337; architecture, 320–21, 368–72, 393–94; of Giuliano, Plate *107*, 321, 339; dating, 325–26; and portraiture, 328–31, 334; iconography, 331, 370, 386–99; names of Dukes, 334–38; of Lorenzo, Plate *106*, 335, 338; setting up of statues, 337–38; setting up of sarcophagus statues, Plate *137*, 364–65; and earlier tombs, 369–70; and architecture, 370. *See also individual works*

Medici *Madonna*, see *Madonna*, Medici Chapel

Moses, Tomb of Julius II, Plate *55*, 131–32, 170, 272; iconography, 132, 173, 276–77; dimensions, 155; and *Laocoön*, 172–73; and Donatello's *St. John*, 173; in plan of *1513*, 173, 174; profile view, Plate *57.2*, 173–74; composition, 174–75; final setting, 175, 186, 276; in plan of *1516*, 175, 191; block, 179; dating, 181; in plan of *1531*, 257–58

Night, Medici Chapel, Plates *100.1, 134.1*, 317–20, 322; drawings, Plates *96, 97.2, 97.3, 97.4*, 313–14; drawing for owl, Plate *68.2*, 314; iconography, 317, 335, 390, 400; rear view, Plate *103.3*, 319; head, Plate *108.1*, 322; profile, Plate *110.4*, 322; dating, 323; legend of

arm, 324n13; mask, Plate *109.3*, 324–25; as ideal type, 329; epigram on, 324n13, 333, 375; and River Gods, 352–54; and scale of sarcophagus, 361; marble block, 362; setting, in original plan, 362–63; and *Leda*, Plate *134*, 365; Tribolo copy, 364; damage to, 365–66; position on sarcophagus, 365–67

Pauline Chapel, 270, 272n10; *Crucifixion of St. Peter*, 278, 279n28
Persian Sibyl, 166n6
Piccolomini Altar, Siena, Plates *28*, *29*, 93–96; and Donatello, 95; study for, 98n2, 108; and *cappelletta*, 158
Pietà, Plate *20*, 60, 67–74; marble, 60, 67–68; and *Bacchus*, 61, 74; head of Virgin, Plates *22.2*, *38.2*, 69, 71, 111; and Verrocchio, 69–71; head of Christ, Plate *22.4*, 71; setting, 72; iconography, 73, 112; drawings after, by Filippino Lippi, Plate *21*, 73–74; and Bruges *Madonna*, 114
Pietà Rondanini, 382n12
Pitti *Madonna, see Madonna*, Pitti
Popes (projected for Medici Chapel), marble for, 308–9
Prophet, Tomb of Julius II, 261, 270–71

Rachel, Plate *79*, 132, 175; iconography, 258, 266, 272, 277; and *Victory*, 266; setting, 276; composition, 278–79; and portaiture, 329, 331
Rebellious Slave, for Tomb of Julius II, Plate *52.1*, 116, 123, 167, 175, 213–17; drawing, Plate *49*, 166; dimensions of base, 169; front view, Plate *57.1*, 170; profile view, Plate *56.2*, 175; and *Dying Slave*, 187, 188; projected setting, 187, 188, 214; and *Christ* of Minerva, 202, 216
River Gods (projected for Medici Chapel), 352–61; marble, 306–9, 356; existing clay model, Plates *99.1*, *101.2*, 309, 319, 352–54, 357; models, 309, 355, 359; drawings, Plates *85.2*, *87*, *94*, *125.1*, *125.2*, *127.1*, 310, 311n1, 314, 353–54, 357, 390–92; iconography, 312, 287–92; in paintings, 353; projected setting, 353–54, 359–60, 370, 392; and tomb of Lorenzo, 354–55; reconstruction, Plate *127.2*, 357; and *Dawn*, 357–58

St. Cosmas, Medici Chapel, Plate *82*, 303
St. Damianus, Medici Chapel, Plate *82*, 303
St. Dominic, shrine, Bologna, 48–53, 149n21. *See also* Angel; *St. Petronius*; *St. Proculus*
St. Gregory, Piccolomini altar, Plate *29.1*, 94–95
St. James, see St. Peter, Piccolomini altar
St. John, Young (lost), 56, 58

St. Matthew, Plate *46*, 10–11, 114, 116, 121–26; and Pitti *Madonna*, 122–23, 126; and *Rebellious Slave*, 123; head, Plate *47.1*, 123–24; and study of satyr, Plate *47.2*, 123–24; and *St. James* of Jacopo Sansovino, Plate *47.3*, 125. *See also* Apostles
St. Paul, Piccolomini altar, Plate *28.2*, 94–95
St. Paul (projected for Tomb of Julius II?), 132
St. Peter (*St. James*), Piccolomini altar, Plate *28.1*, 94–95
St. Peter (projected for Tomb of Julius II?), 136n11, 151n23
St. Petronius, shrine of St. Dominic, Bologna, Plate *12.1*, 49; and Jacopo della Quercia, Plate *13.3*, 50; and late *quattrocento*, 51
St. Pius, Piccolomini altar, Plate *29.2*, *38.4*, *39.4*, 94–95
St. Proculus, shrine of St. Dominic, Bologna, Plate *12.2*, 49; and Niccolò dell'Arca *St. Vitalis*, Plate *13.5*, 51; and Donatello *St. George*, 52; and head of Verrocchio *Colleoni*, Plate *13.1*, 52; and cup of *Bacchus*, 53; and Benedetto da Maiano *Madonna*, Plate *13.4*, 53
Samson and One Philistine, see Victory group, male
Samson and Two Philistines, bronze cast from wax model for Piazza group, Plate *70*, 204, 241–42, 250, 268, 325–26
San Lorenzo, façade, 186, 189–91, 198, 201, 228–29
Sibyls, for Tomb of Julius II, 132, 261, 270–71
Sistine ceiling, 11–13, 126, 217, 219; *Erythrean Sibyl*, 25; *Delphic Sibyl*, Plate *36*, 100, 103, 113, 203; *ignudo*, Plate *53.1*, 126, 149, 171; *putti*, 165; *Persian Sibyl*, 166n6; *Adam*, 331
Slaves, for Tomb of Julius II: studies, 119–20, 166–68, 185, *see also* Tomb of Julius II, drawings; iconography, 130–32, 144–46, 267, 382–83; and herms, 137; architectural function, 144–45; dimensions, 160, 217–18; in plan of *1513*, 166–67; and apes, 169–70; marble blocks, 179; lost, 182–88; in plan of *1519*, 214; in plan of *1532*, 257–59
  Academy: in intermediary plans, 130; as *atlantes*, 145; projected setting, 199–200, 216–19; dating, 200, 216–17; marble block, 201, 202; dimensions, 210; work of assistants, 210–11; iconography, 212–13. *See also* Atlas; *Awakening Captive*; *Bearded Captive*; *Youthful Captive*
  Louvre: unfinished condition, 175; dating, 181–82; and Strozzi family, 182–83, 188; as niche figures, 187–88. *See also Dying Slave*; *Rebellious Slave*
Sleeping Cupid, 56, 58

Taddei *Madonna, see Madonna*, Taddei
Times of Day, Medici Chapel, 316–19; iconography, 268, 312, 331, 388–92; marble blocks, 309; and

Ghiberti's Doors of Paradise, Plate *86*, 311–12, 391; dating, 323; iconography, 329, 330–31; projected setting, Plates *137, 139*, 334–35, 337–38; and poem on death of Giuliano, 335–38, 395; and *Apollo*, 350–51; and River Gods, 352; models, 355–57. *See also Dawn; Day; Evening; Night*

Victory, Plate *74*, 130, 261–69, 279, 325–26, 331; and Danti, Plate *76.2*, 143, 263, 358–59; and Tomb of Julius II, 262–65, 276; and Pierino da Vinci, 263; head, Plate *111.1*, 265, 326; companion piece, 262–63; and *Youthful Slave*, 265–66; and *Apollo*, 350–51

Victory group, male (clay model of two fighting men), Plates *73, 75*, 266–69, 279, 325–26, 331, 343n11; as *Hercules and Cacus*, 245; as *Samson with One Philistine*, 245–46, 266–67; as alleged model for Piazza, 245–49; in plans for Tomb of Julius II, 259–60; as companion piece to *Victory*, 262–63; projected setting, 264; dating, 263–64; iconography, 259

Victory groups, female (projected for Tomb of Julius II): in plan of *1505*, 130, 137; and Bertoldo, 138; and Ghiberti's *Deborah*, Plate *50.4*, 138; and Ammanati *Victory*, Plate *50.1*, 138, 161–64; in plans of *1513*, 51, 137, 138, 153–54; and Donatello's *Judith*, 138, 143; as Virtues, 143, 193, 258–59; iconography, 143–44; number, 146; dimensions, 160–63; marble blocks, 178–79

Youthful Captive, Plate *60.1*, 167, 216; work by assistant, 210–11, 356, 398n19; and *Dying Slave*, 211; wax model, Plates *63.2, 64, 65.2*, 210–11

General Index

Academia Medicea (Platonic Academy), 230–31, 375, 378

Adrian VI, Pope, 190, 221

'Aginensis,' see Rovere, Leonardo Grosso della

Agnolo, Baccio d', model of Tomb of Julius II, 190

Agostino di Duccio, work on marble block for *David*, Plate 25.3, 78–85

Aldovrandi, Giovanni, 48, 201, 202

Algardi, Alessandro, 118

Ammanati, Bartolomeo, 182, 183, 352; *Victory* for tomb of Mario Nari, Plate 50.1, 138, 161–64, 340; *Earth*, Plate 113.3, 340, 345n14; and fountain of Neptune, Plate 126.2, 358

Antiquities: *Antinous*, Plate 25.2, 89, 90; *Apollo Belvedere*, 89, 92, 95, 107; Belvedere torso, Plates 99.2, 100.2, 319, 352; *Caracalla*, bust, 330; *Cupid*, 60n8; *Dead Niobid*, Plate 54.3, 172; *Dionysos*, of Phidias, 390; Hadrian's Tomb, 157; *Hercules Farnese*, copy, 47; *Hercules*, sketch in *Codex Escurialensis*, Plate 11.3, 47; *Hermes Ludovisi*, Plate 44.3, 118; *Horsetamers* (Quirinal), Plate 25.1, 89–90, 92, 107, 119; peplos type of statue, 111; *Laocoön*, Plate 54.2, 171–73, 175, 211, 213; *Okeanos*, Plate 124.3, 354; *putto* of Cardinal Cesi, 119; sarcophagi, arcaded, 141; sarcophagus, Roman, Plate 50.3, 137–38; sarcophagus of Camposanto of Pisa (*Battle of Romans and Barbarians*), Plate 6.2, 40–41; sarcophagus from Pantheon, Plate 141.2, 364; sarcophagus of Villa Borghese, 41; *Venus*, drawing on Chantilly sheet, 67; *Venus*, Cnidian type, 344

Antonio da Pontassieve, 137, 160, 161n2, 176–77, 191, 195, 218, 274

Antonio da Sangallo the Younger, 165n4

Aristotile da Sangallo, see Sangallo, Aristotile da

Baccio d'Agnolo, 190

Baccio da Montelupo, 58, 71, 94n2

Banco, Nanni d'Antonio di, *Isaiah*, Plate 23.1, 78, 81, 83

Bandinelli, Baccio, 125; group for the Piazza, Plates 69.1, 72, 82n13, 237–44, 248–49; *St. Peter*, 238

Barbazza, Bartolomeo, 229

Bartolommeo di Pietro (Baccellino), stonecutter, 79

Basso, Bernardino, mason, 295

Bellini, Giovanni, 208

Benedetto da Maiano, see Maiano, Benedetto da

Benedetto da Rovezzano, 97, 125; tomb of Charles, Duke of Orléans, Plate 50.2, 141–43, 177

Bernardino di Piero Basso, stonecutter, 177

Bernini, Giovanni Lorenzo, 204n29, 372

Bertoldo di Giovanni, 4n5, 13, 27–29, 35–36, 138; *Crucifixion*, Plate 4.1, 27; *Wild Man on Horseback*, Plate 7.1, 28; *Hercules*, Plate 11.4, 28–29; *Arion*, Plate 5.2, 28, 42; *Bellerophon with Pegasus*, Plate 5.1, 28, 42, 90; *Battle of Horsemen*, Plate 6.1, 40–41

Bettini, Domenico (Topolino), 295, 299, 302, 306–8, 356, 362n18, 363n22

Bigio, Nanni di Baccio, 183

Boccacio, Giovanni, 7

Boethius, 396

Bologna, shrine of St. Dominic, 48–55

Boscoli, Tommaso (Maso dal Bosco), 273, 297

Bosse, Abraham, 45

Botticelli, Sandro, 90

BRACCHI, Cecchino, 382n13
Braccio, defined, 44n5
BRAMANTE, Donato, 150–51, 196
BREGNO, Andrea, 93
BRUNELLESCHI, Filippo, 208n42
BRUNI, Lionardo, tomb, 142, 369
BUONARROTI, Buonarroto, 177, 178
BUONARROTI, Gismondo, 255
BUONARROTI, Ludovico, 3
BUONARROTI, Michelangelo, *see* MICHELANGELO Buonarroti; *Index of Works by Michelangelo*
BUONINSEGNI, Domenico, 190, 220, 243, 302, 305n41

CALCAGNI, Tiberio, 398
CANOSSA, Alessandro, Count, 3
Carrata, defined, 178n16, 179nn22–24
CASTAGNO, Andrea del, 369
CATHERINE de'Medici, Queen of France, 182, 332n6
CAVALIERI, Tommaso, 183, 326, 382n13, 387
CELLINI, Benvenuto: *Mercury*, Plate *117.3*, 343; *Minerva*, Plate *118.2*, 344; *Narcissus*, 359n14
CENCI, Bernardo, 200, 205
CHARLES of Orléans, tomb, Plate *50.2*, 141–43, 177
CHIGI, Agostino, 180
Christian theology, and Neoplatonism, 375–81
CLEMENT VII, Pope (Giulio de'Medici), 56; and Tomb of Julius II, 189, 200, 220, 228, 234, 254–55, 269; and Medici Chapel, 191, 220–21, 285–89, 292–94, 306–7, 336–37, 355, 368–69, 395; as patron of Michelangelo, 225, 239–40, 253, 255–56, 261, 348n17; political position, 233–34, 244–45, 255, 294, 332
COLONNA, Cardinal Pompeo, 244
COLONNA, Vittoria, 382n13
Contrapposto, in Michelangelo's works, 10–13, 123, 278–79
CORDIERI, Niccolò, *St. Gregory*, Plate *29.3*, 135–36n11
COSINI, Silvio: assistant on Medici Chapel, 297; frieze of masks, Plate *89.3*, 297–98; serpents, 298; candlestick, Plate *89.2*, 297n19; tomb of Lorenzo, 321; tomb of Ruggiero Minerbetti, Plate *88.3*, 298, 321
CREDI, Lorenzo di, 90
CRONACA (Simone di Pollaiuolo), 99

DALMATA, Giovanni, 227
DAN, Pierre, 45n7
DANIELE da Volterra, 183; *Slaughter of the Innocents* (detail), Plate *71.1*, 241
DANTE Alighieri, 8–9, 230–31; source for *Rachel* and *Leah*, 277, 375, 376; *Divine Comedy*, 378–79; *De Monarchia*, 385

DANTI, Vincenzo: *Honor Overcoming Deceit*, Plates *76.2*, *129.1*, 143, 263, 267, 303, 359; statues for Medici Chapel, 324n10, 358–61
DEINOKRATES of Macedon, 143n20
dell'ARCA, Niccolò, *see* NICCOLÒ dell'Arca
dal BOSCO, Maso (Tommaso Boscoli), 273, 297
del CASTAGNO, Andrea, 369
del CAVALIERE, Tommaso (Tommaso Cavalieri), 183, 326, 382n13, 387
del PIOMBO, Sebastiano, 1, 199, 206–7, 231, 233, 253–56
della PORTA, Giovan Maria, 254, 256n17, 272
della QUERCIA, Jacopo, *see* QUERCIA, Jacopo della
del RICCIO, Luigi, 182
della ROBBIA, Luca, 52
della ROVERE, *see* ROVERE; JULIUS II
della VOLPAIA, Bernardo, 255
DELLO di Niccolò Delli, 208
DESIDERIO da Settignano, 64; *Madonna and Child*, Plate *8.1*, 31–32; tomb of Carlo Marzuppini, Plate *141.1*, 288n14, 296, 369–70
DIONYSOS the Areopagite, 379n5
DONATELLO, 5, 12, 27–36, 85, 94, 110–13; *Crucifixion*, Plate *4.2*, 27; *Judith*, Plates *37.1*, *39.1*, 27, 35, 90, 111–12, 121, 268; *Madonna in the Clouds*, Plate *8.2*, 30–36; San Lorenzo bronze doors, Plate *7.2*, 35; *David*, Plate *23.2*, 78, 81, 83; and Michelangelo *David*, 78–86, 88; *St. Mark*, Plate *28.3*, 94, 124; tomb of Baldassare Coscia, 142; *St. John*, Plate *56.1*, 173
DONI, Angelo, 89, 100
DONI, Anton Francesco, 309, 324n13
Drawings, anonymous: three standing figures, Plate *2.3*, 19–20, 23; *Hercules*, Plate *11.3*, 47; study of Pitti *Madonna*, Plate *48.2*, 113n23; study for a Madonna, Plate *43.3*, 116–17; Hermes group, pupil of Raphael, Plate *44.4*, 118–19; and Tomb of Julius II, plan of *1513*, Plate *51*, 130, 137–38, 158, 160–61, 165–66, 169–70, 173–74, 185, 212; Slave (*1519*), 200n12; and Medici Chapel, Plates *94*, *95*, 302–4, 315, 347, 350n20; ducal monument, Plate *113.4*, 336, 345n15, 347; youth (*Heaven*), Plate *116*, 341–43; copy of dragon, Plate *122.2*, 342n9; youth (*Apollo*), Plate *119.1*, 346–47; *Apollo*, diagonal view, 346–47, 349, 354; torso (*Venus*), Plates *118.3*, *118.6*, 346; anatomical study, Plate *125.1*, 354; Winged Victory, Plate *129.2*, 359n14
Drawings, by Michelangelo. *See Index of Works by Michelangelo*
Drawings, various artists. *See individual artist*
DUQUESNOY, Jerome, copy of *Christ* of Minerva, 204n

DUCERCEAU, Jacques Androuet, engraving of bronze *David*, 97
DÜRER, Albrecht, and Bruges *Madonna*, 115*n*36

Euphuism, 387

FALCONI, Silvio, 176
FANCELLI, Domenico, 177
FANCELLI, Sandro (Scherano da Settignano), 270, 271
FATTUCCI, Giovanni Francesco: and Tomb of Julius II, 221–25, 227, 231–34, 253; and group for Piazza, 239; and Medici Chapel, 294, 302, 305*n*41, 305*n*43, 306
FEDERIGHI, Antonio, *Bacchus*, Plate *25.4*, 51*n*4, 89
FERRUCCI, Andrea, 125; Fiesole altar, Plate *67.3*, 196; and Medici Chapel, 297–98; monument for Antonio Strozzi, Plate *89.1*, 297–98
FIESOLE, Mino da, 227
FIORENTINO, Adriano, 28*n*5
Florence: and *David*, 90–92; Medici rule, 182–83, 244–45, 255, 330–34; and group for Piazza, 237–45, 267
Florentine Academy, 387–88, 402
Fontainebleau, Palace of, and lost *Hercules*, 45–47
FRANCESCO da Sangallo, 297*n*19
FRANCIS I, of France, 182
FRANCO, Battista, *Battle of Montemurlo*, 398*n*20
FRIZZI, Federigo, 205–6, 209

GALLI, Jacopo, 59–61, 93
GENGA, Girolamo, 253–54
GHIBERTI, Lorenzo, Doors of Paradise (details), 21; *Deborah*, Plate *50.4*, 138; Biblical figures, Plate *86*, 311–12, 391
GHIRLANDAIO, Domenico, 3, 6, 19–24, 103; study of two women, Plate *3.1*, 23; *Naming of the Baptist* (detail), Plate *15.1*, 55
GIACOMO da Vignola, church of Sant'Andrea, 133
GIOTTO, *Ascension of St. John* (detail), Plate *1.1*, 17–18
GIOVAN MARIA della Porta, 254, 256*n*17, 272
GIOVANNI da Bologna (Giambologna), 267, 360*n*15
GIULIANO da Sangallo, 90–91, 150*n*22
GOETHE, Johann Wolfgang von, 401
GONDI, Piero, 239
GRANACCI, Francesco, 3–4
GUIDO d'Antonio, stonecutter, 178

Half-baluster, 165*n*4, 296
HEEMSKERCK, Martin, drawings: of *Bacchus*, Plate *19.2*, 62*n*19, 63, 66*n*19, 360; of *putto*, 119; of Belvedere torso, Plate *99.2*, 319

HENRY II, of France, 182–83, 188
HIERONIMO da Urbino, 221, 234

JACOPINO del Conte, 353
JACOPO della Quercia, *see* QUERCIA, Jacopo della
JULIUS II, Pope (Giuliano della Rovere), 1, 108–9, 122, 126, 130–31, 153; decision to build new St. Peter's, 150–51, 239; allusions to in his Tomb, 276–77. *See also Index of Works by Michelangelo*, Julius II, Tomb of

LA GROSLAYE, Cardinal Jean de, 68–69
LANDINI, Taddeo, statue after *Christ* of Minerva, 204*n*28, 207*n*39
LANDUCCI, Luca, 44*n*6
Leda and the Swan (copy), Plate *134.2*, 365
LEO X, Pope (Giovanni de'Medici), 4*n*4, 176, 190, 230–31, 283, 331–32
LEONARDO da Vinci: caricatures, 25; and *David*, 90–92; St. Anne drawings, 101, 104–5
LEONI, Leone, 240
LIPPI, Filippino: *Pietà* drawings, Plate *21*, 73–74; and *David*, 90
LORENZO Monaco, 208
LUCA della Robbia, 52

MAIANO, Benedetto da, 30, 36*n*17; *Madonna and Child*, Plate *13.4*, 53, 115*n*36; *St. Sebastian*, 53; tomb of Filippo Strozzi, Plate *19.3*, 63; *Annunciation* (Naples), 63; Berlin *Madonna*, 71; sculptural style, 71; altar style, 196
MAINARDI, Bastiano, drawing of kneeling figure, Plate *2.4*, 19
MALSPINA, Alberigo, Marchese of Massa, 237
Mannerism, 95, 165, 340, 353*n*5, 358, 361–62, 387
MANTEGNA, Andrea, *Christ*, 71
MARCHESANA, Bona, 293
MARZUPPINI, Carlo, tomb, Plate *141.1*, 288*n*14, 296, 369–70
MASACCIO, *The Tribute Money* (detail), Plate *3.2*, 17–22, 26–27
MASO dal Bosco, *see* Boscoli, Tommaso
Mass of St. Gregory, legend, 209
MATELDA, and Allegories for Tomb of Julius II, 277
MATHAM, Jacob, engraving after *Christ* of Minerva, 204*n*29
MATTEO di Cuccarello, 178–80
MEDICI family, 4*n*5, 30, 48*n*1, 56; political situation, 112, 183, 240, 242, 244–45, 293–94, 331–32, 334, 395; and Strozzi, 182; and Rovere, 191; and Tomb of Julius II, 274; and *Apollo*, 348

MEDICI, Alessandro de', Duke of Florence, 245, 255, 274, 330, 337, 332*n*6, 337; Vasari portrait, Plate *113.5*, 337

MEDICI, Catherine de', Queen of France, 182, 332*n*6

MEDICI, Cosimo I de', Duke of Florence, 4*n*4, 183, 333, 348; and lost statues of Slaves, 182–84, 188; and Academy River God, 352; statue by Danti, 360; statue by Giovanni da Bologna, 360*n*15

MEDICI, Giovanni de', *see* LEO X

MEDICI, Giovanni Bicci de', 141, 369

MEDICI, Giuliano de', (d. *1478*), 285

MEDICI, Giulio de', *see* CLEMENT VII

MEDICI, Giuliano de', Duke of Nemours, 283, 331–34, 332; statue in Medici Chapel, *see Index of Works by Michelangelo, Giuliano*

MEDICI, Cardinal Ippolito de', 245, 348*n*17

MEDICI, Lionardo de', 348

MEDICI, Lorenzino de', and *Brutus*, 330, 331

MEDICI, Lorenzo de' (Il Magnifico), 4–5, 38, 40, 43–44, 230*n*39, 395

MEDICI, Lorenzo de', Duke of Urbino, 4*n*4, 182, 244, 283, 331–34, 332, 337; statue in Medici Chapel, *see Index of Works by Michelangelo, Lorenzo*

MEDICI, Piero de', 44, 59, 141, 332

MEO del Corte, *scarpellino*, 307*n*52

MICHELANGELO Buonarroti: character, 1–2, 5–7, 14, 96, 109, 126, 146, 404; and family, 3, 5, 60; and Ghirlandaio, 3, 6, 17, 23, 24, 103; and Julius II, 3, 97, 108, 150, 153, 239; and Bertoldo, 4, 5, 27, 30; and antiquity, 4, 5, 33, 34, 74, 78, 117–18, 121, 137–38, 171–73, 175, 319, 344–45; and Medici, 4, 43, 44, 56–57, 182, 245, 332–34, *see also* CLEMENT VII, LEO X, MEDICI family, *and individual members of Medici family*; and Donatello, 5, 30–35, 37, 85, 88, 94, 125, 138, 173; and Dante, 9, 231, 378–80; and Masaccio, 21; and *quattrocento*, 22, 51, 61–62, 69, 74, 77, 78, 113; early study of drawing, 24; and Schongauer, 24; and Desiderio, 31, 32; decision to leave Florence, 44; visits Bologna, 48, 125; study of anatomy, 51; first visit to Rome, 56, 58, 120; and Savonarola, 57–58; second visit to Rome, 93, 121, 122, 125, 150, 151; study of painting, 99, 105; and Signorelli, 101–3, 117; and Ghiberti, 138; and Leo X, 189–90; illnesses, 182, 199; death, 183; road to Serravezza quarries, 198; and Clement VII, 224, 225, 234, 253, 255–56; as military architect, 242; style of old age, 279; disposition of works in Florence, 348; and Neoplatonism, 376–78, 380

interpretations: sixteenth-century, 1–2, 6; modern, 6–14, 401; iconography, 6, 387, 399–400; *contrapposto*,

10–13; Platonism, 9, 145, 328, 375, 387–90; Neoplatonism, 9, 375, 380–84, 401–2; of *Leah*, 279; of *Lorenzo* and *Giuliano*, 328, 332–35; *carcere terreno*, 380–82; validity, 399–404

letters: to his family, 5*n*6; to Lorenzo di Pierofrancesco de'Medici, 58; to his father, 59, 109, 114, 115; to Giuliano da Sangallo, 151; concerning Tomb of Julius II, 153*n*1, 156, 189, 220; —, to Buonarroto, 177, 178; —, to Fatucci, 186, 188, 221, 224, 232; —, to Sebastiano del Piombo, 190*n*3; —, to his father, 190; concerning group for the Piazza, to Fatucci, 239, 243; concerning Medici Chapel, 323; —, to Fatucci, 294, 308; —, to Clement VII, 305

opinions: on nature of form, 43; on Northern art, 51; on tradition in art, 69–70; on Donatello's ideal of sculpture, 85; on block, 85, 123, 225–26; on portraiture, 25, 150, 328–30

poetry: on *Night*, quoted, 318; on death of Giuliano de'Medici, 335, 339, 375, 376; —, quoted, 395; *Al cor di zolfo*, 376–77; sonnets, quoted, 377–78, 380; influence of Dante, 379–80

MINI, Antonio, 346

MINI, Giovan Battista, 325, 327, 336

MINO da Fiesole, 227

MONTELUPO, Baccio da, 58, 71, 94*n*2

MONTELUPO, Raffaello da, 270–73, 342*n*9

MONTORSOLI, Giovannantonio, 261; and Medici Chapel, 304, 336–37; tomb of Sannazaro, Plate *112.2*, 345

Mouscrons, of Bruges, 115

NANNI d'Antonio di Banco, *Isaiah*, Plate *23.1*, 78, 81, 83

NANNI di Baccio Bigio, 183

NARI, Mario, tomb, Plate *50.1*, 138, 161–64, 340

Neoplatonism, 9, 375–84

NICCOLINI, Bernardo, 302, 305*n*41

NICCOLÒ dell'Arca, shrine of St. Dominic, Bologna: *St. Agricola*, 18*n*3; and Michelangelo, 49; *St. Vitalis*, Plate *13.5*, 51; *Angel*, Plate *14.1*, 51–52

ORCAGNA, 55

ORLÉANS, Charles, Duke of, tomb, Plate *50.2*, 141–43, 177

ORSINI, Alfonsina, 332

PALLAVICINI, Francesco, 198, 200, 221

PAUL II, Pope (Pietro Barbo), tomb, 224–27

PAUL III, Pope (Alessandro Farnese), 270, 272

PERUGINO, 12, 36, 90

PETRARCH, 375–79, 380–81, 392, 394

Piccolomini, Enea Silvio de (Pius II), tomb, 224–28
Piccolomini, Francesco Todeschini, Cardinal of Siena (Pius III), 93, 96
Pico della Mirandola, Giovanni, 388–89
Piero d'Argento, 60
Piero di Cosimo, 90
Pierino da Vinci: *Samson*, Plate *76.1*, 242*n*18, 263, 267, 303; and Danti, 359
Pietà theme, 68–69
Pietro da Barga, 66*n*19, 204
Pisano, Giovanni, 104, 113
Pisano, Nicola, 49
Pitti, Bartolomeo, 104
Pius II (Enea Silvio de Piccolomini), tomb, 224–28
Pius III, Pope (Francesco Todeschini Piccolomini), 93, 96
Plato, 378–79, 387
Platonic Academy (Academia Medicea), 230–31, 375, 378
Plotinus, 375, 379, 381*n*10
Poliziano, Angelo, 38
Pollaiuolo, Antonio, 86–87, 243*n*22, 369
Pollaiuolo, Simone de (Il Cronaca), 99
Prudentius, 143
Portugal, Cardinal of, tomb, 369–70, 391*n*11
Pucci, Lorenzo, Cardinal of Santi Quattro, 153, 156–57, 176, 221–22

Quercia, Jacopo della: *St. Petronius*, Plate *13.3*, 49; *Genesis* reliefs, 50

Raffaello da Montelupo, 270–73, 342*n*9
Raphael: drawing after *David*, 92, 109; Doni portraits, 100*n*6; and Taddei *Madonna*, 108–9, 111*n*31, 115; *Council of the Gods*, 118; *Meeting with Attila*, 151*n*23; *Castiglione*, 329; *Stanza d'Eliodoro*, 329; ideal of beauty, 401
Riario, Cardinal Raffaele, 58
Robertet, Florimard, 97
Rohan, Pierre de, Sire de Gié, 96, 97
Rome: St. Peter's Basilica, 129, 150–51, 368, 371; San Pietro in Vincoli, 129, 269; San Silvestro in Capite, 229–30
Rosselli, Cosimo di Lorenzo Filippi, 90
Rossellino, Antonio, 63, 80, 83, 196, 391*n*11; tomb of Cardinal of Portugal, Plate *140*, 369–70
Rossellino, Bernardo, 78–79, 142, 150–51, 369
Rovere family, 129, 164, 191, 221–27, 231–34, 253–57
Rovere, Bartolomeo della, 222, 224–25, 231

Rovere, Francesco Maria della, Duke of Urbino, 164, 190–91, 222–25, 253–56, 258, 264, 270, 307, 332
Rovere, Giuliano della, *see* Julius II
Rovere, Guidobaldo II della, Duke of Urbino, 270, 272
Rovere, Leonardo Grosso della, Cardinal of Agen (Aginensis), 153, 156–57, 164, 176, 198–200, 220–22
Rustici, Gianfrancesco, 244

Salviati, Francesco: and Tomb of Julius II, 221, 223; and Medici Chapel, 306; drawing after *Apollo*, Plate *119.4*, 349–50
Salviati, Jacopo, 199
San Biagio in Montepulciano, ground plan, 135*n*9
Sangallo, Antonio the Younger, 165*n*4
Sangallo, Aristotile da: grisaille copy of *Battle of Cascina*, Plate *42.2*, 106–7; drawing of Tomb of Julius II, Plate *81.1*, 194*n*57, 219*n*57, 233, 273–75
Sangallo, Francesco da, 297*n*19
Sangallo, Giuliano da, 90–91, 150*n*22
Sannazaro, Jacopo, tomb, Plate *112.2*, 345
Sansovino, Andrea, 125, 222, 227, 339; and *David*, 80, 85, 90, 92; and Medici Chapel, 316*n*1
Sansovino, Jacopo, *St. James*, Plate *47.3*, 125
Santi Quattro, Cardinal of (Lorenzo Pucci), 153, 156–57, 176, 221–22
Savonarola, Girolamo, 57–58
Scherano da Settignano (Sandro Fancelli), 270, 271
Schongauer, Martin, 23, 25
Sculpture, anonymous: *Mercury*, Plate *117.4*, 344; of River Gods, Plates *124.2*, *128*, 353*n*4, 361, 390
Sebastiano del Piombo, 1, 199, 206–7, 231, 233, 253–56
Sellaio, Leonardo: *Pietà*, 68*n*20; and Tomb of Julius II, 185, 196–99, 221–24, 231–32; and *Christ of Minerva*, 201, 207*n*37; and Medici Chapel, 305–9, 356
Seneca, 381
Signorelli, Luca, 117; *Holy Family*, Plate *32.3*, 101; *Madonna and Child*, Plate *32.4*, 101, 103, 116–17
Silvestre, Israel, etchings of lost *Hercules*, Plates *11.1*, *11.2*, 46
Soderini, Cardinal Antonio, 294
Soderini, Piero, 122, 229–30, 237, 243
Spinelli, Niccolò, 30
Staccoli, Hieronimo, 233, 254–55
Strozzi family: and Doni *Madonna*, 100*n*6; and lost Slaves for Tomb of Julius II, 182–84
Strozzi, Antonio, tomb, Plate *89.1*, 165
Strozzi, Cardinal Roberto, 182–83
Strozzi, Filippo I, 20
Strozzi, Giambattista (Filippo II), 324*n*13, 333, 375
Strozzi, Leone, 183

STROZZI, Maddalena, 100
STROZZI, Piero, 183
STROZZI, Roberto, 182
SUESSA, Duke of, 223

TADDEI, Taddeo, 98
THOMAS AQUINAS, St., 379*n*5
TINTORETTO, 347*n*15
TIRANNO, Girolamo, 270, 272–73
Tombs, types, 139–42, 227, 229, 231, 368–70. *See also individual works*
TOMMASO del Cavaliere (Cavalieri), 183, 326, 382*n*13, 387
Tondo, 100*n*6, 112
TOPOLINO (Domenico Bettini), 295, 299, 302, 356, 362*n*18, 363*n*22
TORRIGIANI, Pietro, 93
TRIBOLO, Niccolò, 146, 242*n*18, 263, 324*n*10, 339; *Victory*, Plate *132.1*, 361; figures on Palazzo del Commune, Prato, Plate *133.1*, 361; clay statuette, Plate *132.2*, 361; copy of *Dawn*, Plate *136.2*, 361, 365–67, 393; copy of *Evening*, Plate *133.2*, 361, 365–67; copy of *Day*, Plate *135.2*, 361–67

URBANO, Pietro, 206
URBINO, Francesco di Bernardino d'Amadore, 272–73, 330*n*2
URBINO, Duchy of, *see* ROVERE; JULIUS II

VALORI, Baccio, 348
VARI, Metello, 200–1, 205, 207
VASARI, Giorgio, portrait of Allessandro de'Medici, Plate 113.5, 337
VERROCCHIO, 29, 62–64, 86–87, 141, 369; *Colleoni*, head, Plate *13.1*, Forteguerri tomb, 64, 71; head of *Faith*, Plate *22.3*, 71
VIGNOLA, Giacomo da, church of Sant'Andrea, 133
VOLTERRA, Daniele da, 183; *Slaughter of the Innocents* (detail), Plate *71.1*, 241